# Discover Woolwich a

# Discover
# WOOLWICH
## and its ENVIRONS

A comprehensive guide to WOOLWICH,
THE ROYAL ARSENAL, WOOLWICH COMMON,
PLUMSTEAD, SHOOTERS HILL & ABBEY WOOD

### by DARRELL SPURGEON

GREENWICH GUIDE-BOOKS

Copyright © Darrell Spurgeon 1996

All rights reserved. No part of this book may be copied or otherwise reproduced, stored in a retrieval system, or transmitted, in any form or by any means, electronic, mechanical, photocopying, recording or otherwise, without the prior permission of the author.

First published in Great Britain 1990 by
Greenwich Guide-Books,
72 Kidbrooke Grove, Blackheath, London SE3 0LG
(phone 0181-858 5831)
Second edition, extensively revised, 1996

Other volumes in the same series by the same author:
Volume I (first edition), covering Woolwich, Plumstead, Shooters Hill, East Wickham, Abbey Wood & Thamesmead (published 1990, out of print)
Volume II, covering Greenwich, Westcombe & Charlton (published 1991)
Volume III, covering Eltham, New Eltham, Mottingham, Grove Park, Kidbrooke & Shooters Hill (published 1992)
Volume IV, covering Bexley, Bexleyheath, Welling, Sidcup, Footscray & North Cray (published 1993)
Volume V, covering Crayford, Slade Green, Erith, Belvedere, Abbey Wood & Thamesmead (published 1995)
In preparation: Brockley, Deptford, New Cross

Front cover photograph is Royal Brass Foundry (1717)
*gazetteer reference Royal Arsenal 3*

Printed in Great Britain by Short Run Press, Exeter

A catalogue record for this book is available from the British Library
ISBN 0 9515624 5 2

# CONTENTS

Foreword   page 7

## WOOLWICH
Introduction   10
Section 'A' (Town Centre)   15
Section 'B' (Riverside & North Woolwich)   21
Section 'C' (West Woolwich)   25
Section 'D' (Thames Barrier & Hanging Wood)   30
Section 'E' (Burrage Town)   34
Suggested Walks   37

## THE ROYAL ARSENAL   41

## WOOLWICH COMMON   49
Suggested Walk   57

## PLUMSTEAD
Introduction   59
Section 'A' (West Plumstead)   60
Section 'B' (Plumstead Common)   62
Section 'C' (Plumstead High Street)   66
Suggested Walk   70

## SHOOTERS HILL
Introduction   72
Section 'A' (Roman Road & Woodlands)   75
Section 'B' (The Northern Slopes)   80
Suggested Walk   82

## ABBEY WOOD
Introduction   85
Section 'A' (Lesnes Abbey & Woods)   87
Section 'B' (Lower Abbey Wood & Bostall)   90

Bibliography   93
Index   94

## MAPS & PLANS
Woolwich & its Environs   6
Woolwich Sections 'A', 'B' & 'E'   14
Woolwich Sections 'C' & 'D'   24
The Royal Arsenal plan   40
Woolwich Common   48
Plumstead general map   58
Shooters Hill general map   74
Abbey Wood general map   84
Lesnes Abbey plan   86

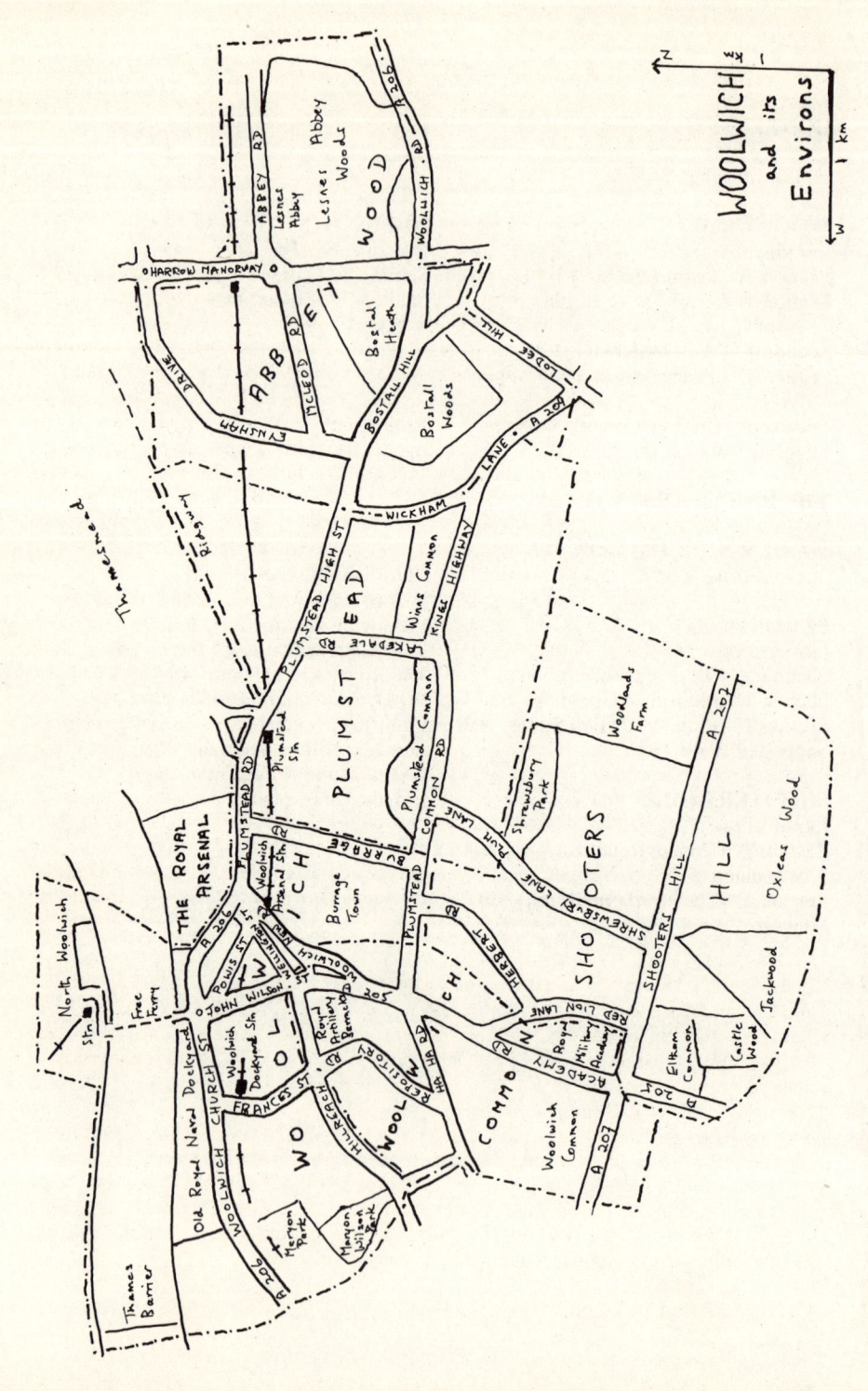

# FOREWORD

The first edition of this book, the original book in the series, appeared in 1990 and sold out within the first year. This new edition has been extensively revised and rewritten. The gazetteers on Woolwich and Plumstead have been enlarged, and there are now twice as many locations as were included in the earlier book. The section on The Royal Arsenal now includes descriptions of all the older buildings on the site. Much new research on the Arsenal and the Dockyard, which was not available six years ago, has been incorporated. The gazetteers on Shooters Hill and Abbey Wood have been updated and include some new locations which were not in earlier books.

To make way, as it were, for the additional text in a book of this size, two areas in the first book have this time been omitted altogether - East Wickham and Thamesmead. However, revised descriptions of these two areas were included in recent books in the series - East Wickham in 'Discover Bexley and Sidcup', published in 1993, and Thamesmead in 'Discover Crayford and Erith', published in 1995.

The book covers six areas - Woolwich, The Royal Arsenal, Woolwich Common, Plumstead, Shooters Hill & Abbey Wood. The boundaries between the areas, which are topographical (rather than administrative) boundaries, are shown on the map opposite. The Royal Arsenal and Woolwich Common are in this edition treated as separate areas - The Royal Arsenal has been for nearly 200 years been physically separated from Woolwich by its wall, and it is only very recently that any public access has become possible; and Woolwich Common is a distinct area, both topographically and through its association with the Royal Artillery.

The areas covered by this book are predominantly in the London Borough of Greenwich, and between 1900 and 1965 were in the Metropolitan Borough of Woolwich. The exceptions are Lesnes Abbey and Lesnes Abbey Woods, which are in the London Borough of Bexley, and were therefore before 1965 in Kent not London; the enclave of North Woolwich, now in the London Borough of Newham; and certain locations in Charlton adjoining Woolwich which were until 1965 in the Metropolitan Borough of Greenwich.

The basic framework for each area consists of a brief introduction, gazetteer, map(s), and (except in the case of The Royal Arsenal and Abbey Wood) suggested walk(s). The introduction to Woolwich also covers The Royal Arsenal and Woolwich Common. Each location in the gazetteers is identified (using location numbers) on a map. There are suggested walks where places of interest are concentrated within an area which makes walking practicable and interesting.

Woolwich is divided into five sections - Section 'A' Town Centre; Section 'B' Riverside & North Woolwich; Section 'C' West Woolwich; Section 'D' Thames Barrier & Hanging Wood; and Section 'E' Burrage Town. There are two maps - one covering Sections 'A', 'B' and 'E', and one covering Sections 'C' and 'D'. There are suggested walks which cover most locations in each section, except Section 'D' where the locations are in a logical sequence quite easy to follow.

## 8 - FOREWORD

For reasons explained above, The Royal Arsenal and Woolwich Common, though clearly part of Woolwich, are treated as separate areas. The Royal Arsenal has its own plan, and the locations in the gazetteer are set out in a sequence which is easy to follow. Woolwich Common has its own map and suggested walk.

Plumstead is divided into three sections - Section 'A' West Plumstead; Section 'B' Plumstead Common; and Section 'C' Plumstead High Street. One map covers all sections, and the suggested walk covers most locations in each section.

Shooters Hill is divided into two sections - Section 'A' Roman Road and Woodlands; and Section 'B' The Northern Slopes. One map covers both sections, and the suggested walk covers most locations.

Abbey Wood is divided into two sections - Section 'A' Lesnes Abbey and Woods; and Section 'B' Lower Abbey Wood and Bostall. One map covers both sections. There are no suggested walks as the locations are in some cases thinly spread over a large area and in other cases very closely concentrated; however, the gazetteer entries in Section 'A' describe a route through the Abbey ruins (for which there is a separate plan) and contain advice on a walk through the Woods.

Although the introductions to the areas contain some historical background, and certain locations have some historical information in indented paragraphs, the guide is not a history of the Woolwich area and makes no pretensions to be a work of local history. Again, although some non-specialist knowledge of architecture is assumed, the guide does not become involved in detailed architectural analysis, and a conscious attempt has been made to avoid architectural jargon. Readers interested in further information on local history and architectural detail may like to consult the list of books at the end of the guide.

The gazetteers are intended as a comprehensive list of buildings and landscape features which are of visual interest, though the choice of places is inevitably very personal. The emphasis is on what is there now, not so much on what has been there in the past, and practical information is given on how best to see each place.

The maps, which are the key to the guide, adopt the same practical approach. Virtually every place mentioned in the text is pinpointed on a map in such a way as to make it easy to find and notice. The maps are indicative and not necessarily to scale, and only show those roads which are likely to be important to the visitor. It is suggested that a more detailed road map of the area be obtained.

The starring system in the gazetteers enables visitors to allocate their time to the best advantage. All locations which are starred are, in my opinion, worth a very special effort to see. The stars are from one to three - three stars are given to locations which are of national importance; two stars to other locations which are of outstanding importance; and one star to locations of particular interest. Most locations however are not starred; this does not mean they are not worth seeing, such places invariably have interesting features and help to make the area distinct.

Italics are used for information on access, for other practical advice, for introductory notes before the walks, and also for cross-referencing. Paragraphs with information of a specifically historical nature are indented.

The sequence of locations in the gazetteers broadly follows the order in the suggested walks, and locations not included in the walks are slotted into the sequence in a way which would make it more convenient for a visit.

## FOREWORD - 9

Some locations are difficult of access, and the guide gives practical information on how to overcome this difficulty. In some cases this may not always be possible, but it is certainly worth trying. In other cases, a certain initiative is demanded; for example, it is usually necessary to phone or call at the clergyman's residence to obtain access to church interiors. In my experience most clergymen are extremely helpful in facilitating this. And many places which are private will not in practice turn away the interested visitor asking permission to view. The text includes contact telephone numbers and/or addresses which may be found helpful in this context.

Of the publications which I have consulted, I wish to make particular mention of 'London 2: South', by Bridget Cherry and Nikolaus Pevsner, in the Penguin Buildings of England series; the Department of the Environment List of Buildings of Architectural & Historic Interest, which can be consulted at the National Monuments Record (London office), 55 Blandford Street, London W1; and the Local List of Buildings published by the Planning Department of the London Borough of Greenwich, which is available in local libraries. Other publications which I have found useful are listed in the bibliography at the end.

I wish to give very special thanks and acknowledgment to numerous local people who helped me in various ways. Julian Watson, Frances Ward and Jennie O'Keeffe at the Greenwich Local History Library, Mycenae Road, Blackheath, dealt courteously and efficiently with my many requests for information. I am particularly grateful to Julian and Frances for the time they devoted to me on so many occasions.

Julian Watson, Barbara Ludlow, and Susan Parker and Andrew Bullivant (of the Woolwich & District Antiquarian Society) all read the draft text in full and offered many useful suggestions and much constructive criticism, which has made a significant contribution to certain parts of the book.

Brigadier Ken Timbers, Historical Secretary of the Royal Artillery Institution, read my text on Woolwich Common, and provided useful information on the Artillery Garrison. Many thanks also to Win Cutler, for information on her recent research on Woolwich Dockyard; Bob Ribbens, the Woolwich Town Centre Manager; Tony Eallett; Jim Packer; Howard Bloch, for information on North Woolwich; Bernadette Gillow, Curator of the Greenwich Borough Museum; Alan Turner, of the Royal Arsenal Historical Society; Michael Wilcinskis, for information on Abbey Wood; Enid Webb, who showed me around St Marys Church Woolwich. Clergymen at many churches were helpful in facilitating my visits, but I would wish to make particular mention of the ministers at St Nicholas Plumstead and at St Patricks Plumstead.

Many thanks also to Jim Pope for invaluable advice on production and design; and to Dave Belle (of Anchor Displays, Eltham) for expert processing of the photographs.

The area covered by this guide, like any urban area, is subject to the process of change, and the situation with regard to the condition and function (or even the existence) of buildings, their accessibility etc can change quite rapidly. However, the information was checked before going to print, and if anyone is misled in any way, I can only offer my apologies.

Darrell Spurgeon,

Blackheath, December 1995

# WOOLWICH

## Introduction

Woolwich was already a large industrial town and a nationally important military centre by the time the expansion of the London conurbation reached the area in the late 19th century.

Because of its historical background, its military associations and its riverside site, Woolwich still retains a separate identity as a town, and has not merely been swallowed up by the growth of London.

### Early history

Two burial mounds from the Bronze age have survived nearby, at Plumstead and at Shooters Hill. Evidence of an important late Iron Age defensive settlement and of a Roman camp has been found on the former Woolwich Power Station site. The remains of Roman cemeteries have been discovered in the Royal Arsenal, and remains of Roman burials in Plumstead - at Wickham Lane and near St Nicholas Church. Up to 400 AD there was a substantial Romano-British settlement around the ridge to the west of Maryon Park in Charlton. Many finds from these sites are in Greenwich Borough Museum.

There was a Saxon settlement at Woolwich, as recorded in a charter of 964. By the early medieval period it had become a small riverside village between the river and the present Woolwich High Street, sustained by fishing and a river crossing point, with sandpits to the south. There was a church on the hill to the west by 1115.

### Dockyard and Arsenal, and the industrial town

The first stage in the transformation of Woolwich was the foundation by Henry VIII in 1512 of a shipyard in the western part of the Power Station site. In 1546 the Royal Naval Dockyard was set up on a site to the west below the church, and most subsequent expansion took place further west. The original shipyard became a gun wharf, linked to the Dockyard; a ropeyard was established c1575 to the south along the line of the present Beresford Street.

In the area now covered by the Waterfront Leisure Centre there were pottery and tile kilns in the 16th and 17th centuries. A 17th century kiln for the production of salt-glazed stoneware, the earliest known in Britain, as well as a 17th century earthenware kiln, were discovered during excavations in 1974; the stoneware kiln has been preserved for future display in the Borough Museum. Glass Yard, to the west of the Leisure Centre, marks the site of a 17th century glassworks.

At the end of the 17th century the establishment of the Royal Arsenal to the east on a site originally called The Warren ensured that Woolwich became an important industrial town. The growth of the Arsenal over the next 200 years was on a scale which can only be described as phenomenal.

Both Dockyard and Arsenal now belong to the past. The Dockyard closed in 1869, and the site now has a variety of uses, though some of the 18th and 19th century buildings have been preserved. After the last war activity at the Arsenal declined dramatically, and the Arsenal finally closed at the end of 1994. Though much has been demolished since the last war, the site still contains one of the most important collections of industrial buildings of the 18th and 19th centuries in the country.

Apart from the Dockyard and the Arsenal, the most important industry in the area has been the Siemens factory for the manufacture of submarine cables, which was founded in 1863 and by the end of the last war covered a large area to the west of the Dockyard; it closed in 1968, and the site is now taken up by industrial estates.

## The Thames Barrier

Other industrial activity has been on a relatively small scale. However, a notable event was the construction of the Thames Barrier 1972-83, to counter the ever increasing threat of a serious flood in riverside areas of Central and East London.

The Barrier is actually in the industrial zone of New Charlton. The gazetteers which follow also cover some other locations in Charlton which are on the fringes of Woolwich, including Charlton Cemetery; residential streets which were developed on the former estate of the Maryon-Wilson family, who lived at Charlton House; and parts of the ancient Hanging Wood which also once formed part of the Maryon-Wilson estate.

## Woolwich Common, the Royal Artillery, and the Academy

The Royal Regiment of Artillery was founded in the Arsenal grounds in 1716. The site was later found too restricted, and the Board of Ordnance purchased farmland facing Woolwich Common for construction of a new barracks which started in 1776. Woolwich New Road had been constructed from 1774 to link the two areas.

By 1802 the long and impressive frontage of the barracks had been completed. More space became needed for drill and practice, and in 1802-06 the Board purchased full rights to the use of Woolwich Common. In 1806 Little Heath, Hillreach and Artillery Place were laid out to form a new main road from Charlton to Woolwich, as the road across the Common was often closed for artillery practice.

The expansion of the Artillery led to increased military enclosure of parts of the Common. By 1810 the Royal Artillery area on the Common consisted of the Barracks and the Barrack Field in front, and to the west the Gun Park and the training and storage area known as the Royal Military Repository.

The Royal Military Academy also started life in the Arsenal grounds, in 1741. A large new building for the Academy on the opposite side of Woolwich Common from the Artillery Barracks was completed in 1806. The Academy itself moved to Sandhurst after the last war, and the buildings now form part of the Artillery garrison.

Both the Artillery Barracks and the old Academy retain their original facades; they have a powerful impact on the southern approach to Woolwich, and dominate the vast open space of the Common. On the Common are many other buildings and monuments associated with the Artillery, including the extraordinary Rotunda which at present houses the Museum of Artillery.

In the 19th century there were many other barracks and military establishments around Woolwich Common. This was the heyday of Woolwich as a military centre. Now most of these buildings have gone, but there are some survivals, including Connaught Barracks, the gateways of Red and Cambridge Barracks, and some lengthy stretches of brick wall.

## The growth of housing

There were many houses in the centre of Woolwich by the 1820s, but largescale housing development really began in the 1840s, stimulated by the growth of employment at the Dockyard and at the Arsenal. Two housing areas are of special interest - the hilly streets south of the Dockyard (of this little remains apart from a number of imposing houses in and around Woodhill); and on a larger scale, the hilly streets south of the Arsenal, the area called Burrage Town, which was mostly in the old parish of Plumstead (of this a large part survives). Both these areas were fully built up by the 1860s, and by this period Woolwich had become a substantial town.

The railway reached Woolwich in 1849, adding to the pace of development. Two stations were opened, Woolwich Dockyard and Woolwich Arsenal, both on the site of former sandpits. The railway line now runs through Woolwich in a series of cuttings and tunnels.

Since the war a large number of housing estates have been built both east and west of the town centre, including an estate in the Dockyard site and other estates on the sites of former barracks. To the south is the large Woolwich Common Estate.

## Victorian institutions

A number of well-known institutions founded in the Victorian era are linked with Woolwich - the Woolwich Building Society, founded 1847, its head office now in Bexleyheath; the Royal Arsenal Co-operative Society, founded 1868, now part of the Co-operative Wholesale Society; the Woolwich Arsenal Football Club *(see below)*, founded 1886, known as the Arsenal since it moved to Highbury in 1913; the Woolwich Polytechnic, founded 1890, now the University of Greenwich; and the Woolwich Free Ferry, inaugurated 1889.

## Arsenal Football Club

The Woolwich Arsenal Football Club was founded as Dial Square Football Club by Royal Arsenal workers at the Prince of Wales pub on Plumstead Common in 1886; later that year the name was changed to the Royal Arsenal Football Club at a meeting at the Royal Oak pub (now called the Pullman) in Woolwich. The club first played on Winns Common, then from 1887-88 at two adjacent grounds on Plumstead Marshes near Griffin Manorway, from 1890-91 at grounds at Hector Street, Plumstead, and from 1893-94 back to one of the grounds near Griffin Manorway, when the name was changed to Woolwich Arsenal Football Club. The club moved away to Highbury in 1913 and then became known as Arsenal Football Club.

## The town centre

Powis Street was laid out c1798, and by 1810 many shops had opened there. It was rebuilt with much grander buildings from the 1890s. By this time the expansion of the built-up area of London had reached Woolwich, and the shopping centre had become established in Powis Street, Hare Street and around Beresford Square. Even from 1840, and right up to 1939, it was the largest shopping centre in the region, attracting people from miles around.

The town hall built in Calderwood Street in 1842 still survives. Around the turn of the century other public buildings appeared nearby - the library, the baths, and the Polytechnic. In 1906 a new Town Hall, initially of the Metropolitan Borough of Woolwich and since 1965 of the London Borough of Greenwich, was built in Wellington Street. The police station and magistrates court followed a few years later in Market Street. The area now constitutes the civic centre of Woolwich, with a distinct Edwardian architectural character.

In the 1960s and 1970s a number of large office blocks were built in the Woolwich Town Centre - Riverside House and Churchill House in the 1960s, followed by Miller Freeman House, Crown Buildings, Peggy Middleton House, and Civic House. These have now established Woolwich as an important office centre. However, the importance of Woolwich as a shopping centre has declined substantially.

## Woolwich - the Future

Much effort is being devoted by the Borough Council, working together with the University of Greenwich, the Royal Artillery, local businesses and community organisations etc, to arrest this decline and regenerate the Woolwich area. Already environmental improvements are under way in Powis Street, and hopefully this will be extended soon to Beresford Square.

The ultimate success of these efforts will depend on the future use of the Royal Arsenal site, and how it can be integrated into the Town Centre, given the barrier formed by the main road (A206). The Arsenal site contains a wealth of historically important industrial buildings; their preservation and public access to them are of paramount national importance. Although the Ministry of Defence vacated the site at the end of 1994, it is by no means clear when or even if ready public access will be permitted; in fact, towards the end of 1995 the Royal Artillery moved into a large area at the eastern end of the site, and are likely to stay there until 1998. However, by 1998 there should be public access to some of the more important buildings at the western end, which are earmarked for use by the Royal Artillery Heritage Museum, and by Greenwich Borough Museum and Local History Library. There is however at present no clear picture at all of what will happen to the remainder of the site.

Woolwich deserves to be more widely known and visited. Sensitive usage of (and public access to) the Arsenal site and imaginative development of the riverside, with extension of the riverside walk, are vital and would complement the already existing attractions - the magnificent military buildings on the Common, the Thames Barrier, the Free Ferry. The improvement of public transport links, including two schemes already proposed - the Woolwich Rail Tunnel linking North Woolwich Station under the river with Woolwich Arsenal Station, and the Greenwich to Thamesmead riverside tramlink - would also help. If all this could be realised, the Woolwich area would be more widely regarded as one of the most interesting outlying parts of London, and would become an important tourist destination.

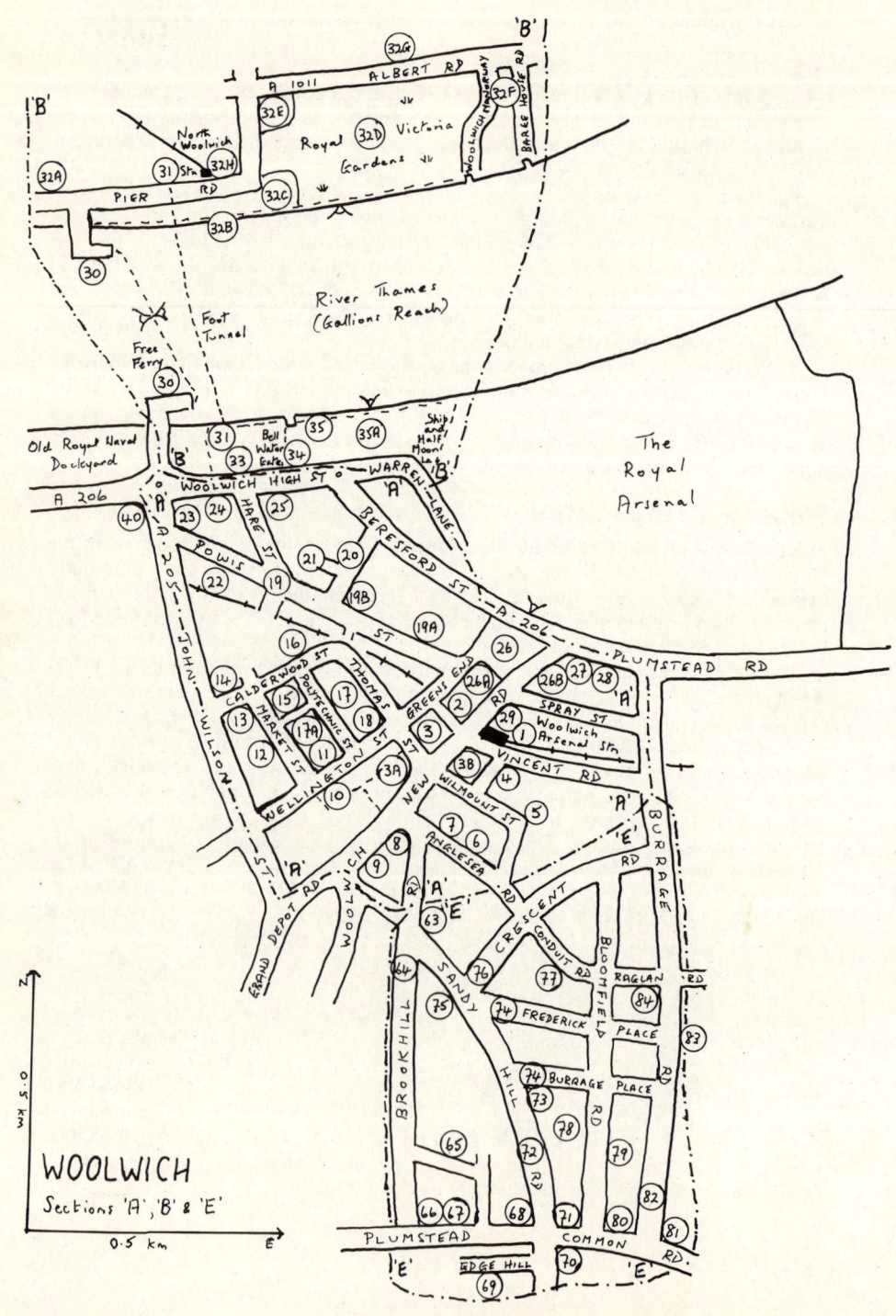

# WOOLWICH

## Gazetteer

### Section 'A' TOWN CENTRE

**1. Woolwich Arsenal Station** was originally opened in 1849 on part of a former sandpit known as Pattisons Pit, which extended as far south as Crescent Road. The present station is an amazing high-tech structure of 1993, which replaced a building of 1905. It has a horseshoe-shaped canopied roof, projecting through which is a circular glass drum like a lighthouse intended to emphasise its site on the corner of the square. The rounded tapering columns clad in Portland stone hide a black steel structure which emerges above the columns to support the canopy, and are fixed to the steel by bolts in visible holes.

On the platforms, the canopies with iron columns remain from the previous building. On the 'up' platform is a terracotta relief sculpture by Martin Williams 1993, 'Workers of Woolwich', depicting workers carrying out processes in the production of weapons and armaments at the Arsenal. The 'up' trains continue through a tunnel 123 metres long under General Gordon Place.

**2. Equitable House**, the old head office of the **Woolwich Building Society**, built 1935. The building is imposing, in an Edwardian baroque style with a mix of art deco motifs. The entrance is flanked by Ionic columns, and there are all sorts of decorative flourishes and features worth noting. There is a splendid art deco banking hall.

> The Woolwich Equitable Building Society was founded at 145 Powis Street in 1847; it started opening branch offices in 1920. The head office moved here in 1935, and from here to a new head office building in Bexleyheath in 1989.

**3. General Gordon Place.** A pleasant landscaped area, which serves as a welcome green space and a focal point for the town centre. It was opened in 1983, the fortuitous result of a redevelopment scheme which aborted.

On the north side are Equitable House and Woolwich Arsenal Station *(see above)*. On the south side is **Woolwich Post Office (3A)**, a fine large red brick building c1892 with some nice terracotta decoration; the single storey curved extension is the sorting office, of the 1920s. Adjoining the Post Office is **1/5 Thomas Street**, an attractive classical group probably c1850 (with altered ground floors). The modernist block to the west is Churchill House, c1964, part of Greenwich University.

A small retail development **(3B)** was built in 1989 on the east side - in a passage leading to the supermarket is a long and colourful mural, by the Greenwich Mural Workshop c1990, depicting the Arsenal gatehouse with Asian market and other scenes. Adjoining is the **Eauzone**, a night-club formerly known as **The Tram Shed**, converted in the 1970s from an old electricity sub-station of 1908 which generated power for the tramways; the internal decor of the Eauzone is quite bizarre.

**4. The Bull**, 14 Vincent Road. An attractive pub, probably c1850, neatly rounding the corner.

**5. A Gurdwara**, or Sikh Temple, of the **Ramgarhia Association**. This powerful building of 1889 with a very classical frontage was originally the Freemasons Hall; it later became the Woolwich Town & Social Club, a workingmens club.

**6. Woolwich & District Synagogue**, Anglesea Road. A modest white modernist building of 1962, raked up steeply to the rear.

**7. Old Carmel Chapel**, Anglesea Road. This large and rather heavy building, with its great round-headed windows above great round-headed doors, was an early Baptist chapel of 1856. It is now disused and its future uncertain.

**8. Anglesea Arms**, 91 Woolwich New Road. An attractive classical pub, probably c1850, with pedimented upper floor windows.

**9. *Church of St Peter the Apostle**, Woolwich New Road. A Roman Catholic church of 1843 in a very positive Victorian Gothic style by the pioneering Gothic Revival architect Augustus Pugin.

Pugin's church consisted of the present nave, aisles and the Lady Chapel (at the end of the north aisle, so originally projecting beyond the east end). The present chancel and St Josephs Chapel (at the end of the south aisle) were added in authentic Pugin style in 1889. The multi-cusped arch to the southern side entrance is particularly pretty; a planned tower over this entrance was never built. Both east and west windows are large and impressive.

The ***interior**, with its acutely pointed arches, is imposing. *(The church is often open, otherwise call at the Presbytery next door, or telephone 0181-854 0359.)* Note the Victorian stained glass in the Lady Chapel by William Wailes; the elaborate Gothic reredos in the chancel, actually of 1942; the ornamental font in St Josephs Chapel; the Stations of the Cross, removed here in 1895 from St Georges Cathedral Southwark; and the modern stone altar, lectern and priest's chair of 1993.

The church, flanked by the presbytery and community centre, form a fine Victorian Gothic complex. The **presbytery** next door at 103/5 Woolwich New Road consists of a small building of 1849 by Pugin, and a larger addition of 1870 by his son Edward Pugin with extraordinary decorative features. The **community centre** to the south was originally a school; the main part was built 1858, with extensions to the rear of 1870 and to the front of 1894.

**10. Director-General**, 55 Wellington Street. This pub, originally of 1863, has an agreeable frontage c1901 with embossed tiles. The interior is attractive; the large room at the back was once used for music-hall performances.

**11. *Town Hall**, Wellington Street. An ornate building of red brick and Portland stone, with a tall clock tower (reminiscent of external features of St Pauls Cathedral). It was built by Sir Alfred Brumwell Thomas (whose other major work was Belfast City Hall) for the Metropolitan Borough of Woolwich in 1906, and became the Town Hall for the London Borough of Greenwich in 1965. It is in the High Edwardian

Baroque style, and has a profusion of columns, pediments, niches, Venetian windows, small circular windows, quoins, balustrades etc. The architectural detailing of both exterior and interior is outstanding.

The entrance porch in Wellington Street projects forward on Ionic columns, and above is a range of 14 larger Ionic columns. The great tower is of red brick, receding to a stage with projecting Ionic columns; near the base, facing Market Street, is a pedimented balcony (known as the Mayor's Balcony) with Ionic columns, supported by two cherubs holding the coat of arms of the Metropolitan Borough of Woolwich. Alongside the tower is a large dome, and behind are three smaller domes. Along Market Street three Venetian windows lead to the entrance to the public hall, which has very profuse decoration under a large pediment.

*Interior. The entrance in Wellington Street leads into the Victoria Hall, which has fine plasterwork and a statue of Queen Victoria by Frederick Pomeroy (funded by public subscription). The first floor galleries round the hall lead to the council chamber and committee rooms, which have fine wood panelling and plasterwork.

Many rooms have stained glass windows by Geoffrey Webb featuring local historical figures and associations. The main ones are: in the Victoria Hall - 'The Sovereign of the Seas'; in the council chamber - Henry VIII & Elizabeth I; in the committee room suite - Sir Thomas More & Margaret Roper, Edward III & King John of France, Phineas Pett & Samuel Pepys; in the public hall - Lovelace 'the cavalier poet', Henry Maudslay, & General Gordon.

**12. 24/28 Market Street.** An early 19th century terrace of small houses, originally part of a longer terrace, an amazing survival in this predominantly Edwardian area.

**13. Woolwich Police Station**, a plain but pleasing building of 1910. Opposite is the **Magistrates Court**, a neo-Georgian building of 1912.

**14. A Gurdwara** (Sikh Temple), Calderwood Street. A large classical building of 1816 with a bold Tuscan portico, and a great series of round-headed windows in round-arched recesses. It was originally the Methodist Chapel for the Artillery Garrison; the mid 19th century building next door was the Wesleyan Methodist Sunday School. Adjoining are 2/3 Calderwood Street, an early 19th century pair.

**15. Old Town Hall**, Calderwood Street. A classical building of 1842, with rusticated ground floor; note the fine lamp-holder over the entrance. It had been the Woolwich Town Hall until 1906. The rear extension along Polytechnic Street is probably of the 1870s.

Adjoining (and on the site of the first Town Hall 1840-42) is **Woolwich Library**, built 1901 by the Woolwich architect Henry Hudson Church, with a great rounded window on the ground floor and a pediment at the top.

**16. Miller Freeman House**, Calderwood Street, formerly known as Morgan Grampian House. A modernist block of 1972, a long slab with a shorter slab at right angles, by Sir John Burnet, Tait & Partners, architects of many such office blocks in Central London..

**17. University of Greenwich**, formerly known as the **Thames Polytechnic**. This is the main campus of the University, a complex occupying virtually an entire block.

## 18 - WOOLWICH

The Woolwich Polytechnic was founded in 1890; it was the first to be established in the country after the original Regent Street Polytechnic. In 1969 it was renamed the Thames Polytechnic. In 1992 it became the main campus of the University of Greenwich, which has other campuses at Avery Hill (Eltham), Dartford, Chatham, West Malling, Deptford and Roehampton, with a total of 17,000 students. It is a regional university for South East London and North & West Kent. There are approx 8000 students at Woolwich, studying mainly science, technology, humanities and business.

The complex contains buildings of different periods in a variety of architectural styles; Bank House, only recently absorbed into the University, is the only building which was not purpose-built.

The original building of 1891, by the Woolwich architect Henry Hudson Church, with gabled dormers and terracotta piers, is in Calderwood Street; the inscription 'Woolwich Polytechnic Young Men's Christian Institute' is over the original entrance, now replaced by a window. Incorporated in the range along Polytechnic Street is the entrance facade of 1898, also with a doorway replaced by a window; this facade is long and symmetrical, and has two oriel windows, some quite fantastic stonework and other ornamental detail. At the corner of Calderwood Street and Thomas Street is the splendid great baroque entrance of 1915, its frontispiece flanked by Ionic columns; behind is the foyer, a rotunda in a well, with circular balustrades in two upper floors receding up to an elegant glazed dome, the most interesting architectural feature of the complex. At the corner of Calderwood Street and Polytechnic Street is the Main Hall, built in 1935. The present main entrance block, a modernist building of 1964, is in Wellington Street. At the junction of Wellington Street and Thomas Street, is Bank House, the former Barclays Bank building c1880, classical with a prominent turret and pilasters.

In the middle of the complex are two courtyards (one a car park, the other largely built over), separated by the library.

The old **Woolwich Baths (17A)** on Bathway, by Henry Hudson Church 1894, with its elaborate but symmetrical facade and a tower, is now the Students Union.

**18. Earl of Chatham**, Thomas Street. A handsome late 19th century pub, the ground floor having a large recessed bay window. Note the abundant Victorian tiling.

**19. Powis Street.** The main shopping street of Woolwich, now pedestrianised. A face-lift scheme for the pedestrianised area has recently started. First laid out c1798, largely rebuilt with grander buildings between 1890 and 1910. Many of the shops retain late Victorian or Edwardian frontages above ground level; Hare Street to the north follows a very similar pattern. Note in Powis Street:

No 12 (19A), the former **William Shakespeare** pub, its present curious facade of c1894. The ground floor has been altered and spoiled, but above note the pillars topped by urns, the Shakespeare bust and a monkey right on top.

Nos 68/86 (19B), formerly Garretts Department Store of 1898, has a substantial unified upper floor, decorated with the Invicta horse of Kent and lots of classical embellishments.

*For the old Co-op building and Granada Cinema in Powis Street, see page 19.*

**20. McBean Street** has lots of passages with older workshop type buildings. The Greenwich Mural Workshop *(see 3B, 25)* is located here. At the junction with Beresford Street is **Woolwich Polytechnic Lower School**, built by the London School Board 1884, large, bulky, and multi-gabled.

21. **Callis Yard**, Bunton Street. This council depot retains, at the end of the courtyard, the old municipal stables of the 1890s. The wide staircase was originally a ramp leading to the first floor where the horses were housed. In the roof, which has a glazed strip along the ridge, was a hay-loft. The horse-keeper's house was the other side of the staircase.

22. **125/161 Powis Street**, the old head office of the **Royal Arsenal Co-operative Society**, a long symmetrical brick and terracotta building of 1903 in Italian Renaissance style, inscribed 'Central Stores', with a prominent clock tower. The terracotta decoration is extraordinarily elaborate and almost riotous.

Over the entrance is a statue by Alfred Drury of Alexander Mcleod, a founder and first full-time secretary, and the Co-op motto 'each for all and all for each'. In the foyer is a foundation plaque and a first world war memorial. The building is now used as offices by the London Borough of Greenwich.

> The RACS was founded by Royal Arsenal workers in 1868 as the Royal Arsenal Supply Association. The first meeting was at The Lord Raglan *(see 84)*; it first traded from a house at 11 Eleanor Road, now Barnard Close, and from 1869 from a house at 29 Parry Place. It was renamed the Royal Arsenal Co-operative Society in 1872; the first RACS shop was opened on this site at 147 Powis Street in 1873.
>
> The RACS became one of the largest retail co-ops in the country. Many services provided to its members were pioneering advances of the time, including libraries, adult education, and with the construction of the Bostall Estate *(see Abbey Wood 11)* 1900-14, low cost housing. Shornells on Bostall Heath *(see Abbey Wood 13B)* was purchased as an education and training centre 1919. Woodlands Farm *(see Shooters Hill 15)* was acquired 1920. The Well Hall Estate at Eltham was purchased 1925 for additional low-cost housing and was renamed Progress Estate. Commonwealth Buildings *(see 42)* was acquired as a warehouse and works area 1926.
>
> The RACS was absorbed by the Manchester-based CWS (Co-operative Wholesale Society) in 1985.

The CWS regional office and store is in the building of 1938, **136/152 Powis Street**, opposite; it is in art deco style with bands of cream faience and continuous windows, and a tall tower with a tall and narrow vertical window. Note that the railings of the internal staircase incorporate the word Co-op. Near the top of no 134 next door are the words 'each for all and all for each' within a wreath.

23. **The Old Granada**, a cinema of 1937, now Gala bingo hall. The stark curved brick exterior hides a quite fantastic *interior (access by joining the bingo club one day beforehand)* by Theodore Komisarjevsky, a sort of Hollywood theatrical extravaganza, using mainly Gothic, but also classical and romanesque motifs.

The entrance foyer with its zigzag-pattern Corinthian columns gives one a hint of what to expect. This leads into the main foyer, surrounded by a gallery with fine railings, and with a roof of carved wooden panels. Steps lead from the main foyer down to the auditorium, but first proceed ahead up the grand staircase to the gallery. On the landing is an arcade of acutely pointed arches, flanked at both ends by two panels with pre-Raphaelite murals. Off the gallery is the hall of mirrors, with rows of trefoiled mirrors and Corinthian columns, and a low fantastically decorated ceiling.

The auditorium is accessed from the main foyer, or from the hall of mirrors into the circle. Beyond the circle it is like a lofty Gothic cathedral, with all sorts of arches, screens and arcades, great romanesque portals flanked by lion and unicorn murals, and a carved wooden panelled ceiling like a medieval Italian palazzo. There are fantastic decorative details everywhere, difficult to take in unless studied carefully.

**24. The Coopers Arms**, 120 Woolwich High Street, formerly known as Plaisteds. Said to be basically of 1790, the oldest pub in Woolwich; and the cellars may be of this date. The present building is of late 19th century appearance, with a well-designed timber ground floor. There is a fine lantern in front inscribed Plaisteds Wine House, and two similar but smaller lanterns along the alley to the side.

Adjoining are **121/123 Woolwich High Street**, basically late 18th century, though much altered and rebuilt, and with modern shopfronts. Note the double mansard roof.

**25. 108/112 Woolwich High Street.** Nos 108/110 are probably early 19th century. Nos 111/2 are probably late 18th century, though in poor condition.

On the side of no 108 is a large mural, 'People of Greenwich, Unite against Racism', by the Greenwich Mural Workshop 1981.

**26. *Beresford Square.** This square, now traffic-free, was up to 1939 often the scene of meetings and popular demonstrations. It has a very lively street market, established officially on this site in 1888.

Dominating the square is the old ***Royal Arsenal Gatehouse**, or Beresford Gate, cut off since 1986 from the Royal Arsenal site by a major road (the A206). The gateway itself and the adjoining gatehouses were built in 1829, the Bell Tower in 1859, and the upper storey over the gateway in 1891. The Gatehouse has recently been restored, and will be converted to offices. Mortars (cast in the Royal Brass Foundry and bearing the royal cipher of George IV) which were on top of the gatehouses have been removed to Fort Nelson, Portsmouth; they will probably be replaced by replicas. To the side of the building is a drinking trough of 1886.

South of the square, note **18/19 Greens End (26A)** - above the modern pub and shop on the ground floor are the upper storeys and mansard roof of an early 18th century house. Next door **20 Greens End**, now Lloyds Bank, has an amazing facade of 1905, with upper floor Ionic columns and ground floor twisted columns, and other classical features and flourishes.

To the east is **15/19 Beresford Square**, a harmonious classical group c1880 with pilasters and end turrets, incorporating the pub **The Ordnance Arms**. It forms an island block of great character, its rear showing similar features and facing

**1/11 Woolwich New Road (26B)**, another imposing late Victorian terrace. No 3 was the home of the Labour Movement in Woolwich from 1904 to the 1970s - the Pioneer Press was set up here (publishing the weekly Labour journal 'The Pioneer') in 1904, and the office of the Labour Representation Association in 1905, which became Woolwich Labour Party in 1916.

**27. The Woolwich Infant**, 9 Plumstead Road. This pub, rebuilt in 1906, has nice etched glass in recessed bay windows. Note the inn-sign on the front wall, showing the bulky gun called the Woolwich Infant *(see also Woolwich Common 20)*.

**28. Cambridge House**, 23 Plumstead Road. A house c1840 with some good decorative features, but now in rather poor condition.

**29. 15/27 Woolwich New Road.** An interesting terraced group - no 15 is basically late 18th century with a mansard roof; no 17 mid 19th century Italianate; nos 19/25 late 19th century (nos 23/25 with a well-preserved shopfront). No 27 is **The Pullman**, a handsome Edwardian pub, recently restored, formerly known as the Royal Oak.

# WOOLWICH

## Gazetteer

### Section 'B' RIVERSIDE & NORTH WOOLWICH
*(See map on page 14)*

**30. \*\*Woolwich Free Ferry**
The ferry takes only a few minutes to cross between Woolwich and North Woolwich. It provides extensive views eastwards along Gallions Reach past the Royal Arsenal towards Thamesmead, and westwards along Woolwich Reach to the Thames Barrier, with the tall buildings of Central London visible in the distance.

> There are records of legal rights to ferries going back to the 14th century, and several ferries operated over the centuries, but always at a charge. The Great Eastern Railway had operated a toll ferry from North Woolwich pier to a pier just east of Bell Watergate from 1847. It persisted until 1908 despite the inauguration in 1889 of the Free Ferry by the London County Council. The Free Ferry used the famous paddle steamers from 1889 to 1963, when drive-on drive-off diesel boats, built at the Caledon shipyard at Dundee, were introduced. Since 1986 the service has been operated by the London Borough of Greenwich.

The three drive-on drive-off ferries (named after Labour Movement figures John Burns and Ernest Bevin and local politician James Newman) were introduced in 1963; the new terminals opened in 1966. The ferry had previously been at the end of Hare Street.

> Services Monday to Friday 0600 - 2030 approx every 10 minutes; Saturday 0600 - 2000 approx every 20 minutes; Sunday 1130 - 1930 approx every 20 minutes; Bank Holidays 0600 - 2000 approx every 20 minutes; no service Xmas Day, Boxing Day, New Years Day.

**31. Woolwich Foot Tunnel**, accessible from Glass Yard (to the west of the Waterfront Leisure Centre) and from the Riverside Walk. The tunnel, 500 metres in length, was built 1909-12 by Sir Maurice Fitzmaurice for the London County Council. As at the Greenwich Foot Tunnel (which was opened ten years earlier), there are similar (and rather elegant) circular entrance buildings with spiky porches on both sides of the river.

> Access to the tunnel is by lift or by long flights of stairs. Open Monday to Saturday 0730 - 1800, Sunday 0900 - 1630. No service Xmas Day, Boxing Day. For visiting North Woolwich, although the tunnel has security camera control, it is probably more pleasant to use the Free Ferry.

**32. \*North Woolwich.** This enclave on the north bank of the river was originally in Woolwich parish; it was part of the Metropolitan Borough of Woolwich from 1900 to 1965, when it became part of the London Borough of Newham. It can be reached by the Free Ferry or the Foot Tunnel.

## 22 - WOOLWICH

In the early 1840s the area round North Woolwich was entirely marshland, with a track which led from East Ham to the river for a ferry to Woolwich. The first station was opened in 1847, probably within the area of the present park, by the Eastern Counties Railway (which became the Great Eastern Railway in 1862); it connected with a ferry from North Woolwich pier, providing a relatively quick journey from Shoreditch to Woolwich. But in 1849 the South Eastern Railway opened its line from London Bridge to Woolwich Dockyard and Woolwich Arsenal, providing a faster service.

So the Railway opened the Pavilion Gardens in 1851 to attract new passengers; this became the Royal Pavilion Gardens in 1852, a pleasure garden with dancing (indoor & open air), theatre, maze, rifle range etc. A new and rather grand station was opened in 1854. (The gardens became a public park, Royal Victoria Gardens, opened by the London County Council in 1890.)

However, the growth of North Woolwich only really began with the development of the Royal Docks from 1855 and Henleys electric telegraph works from the 1860s. The Royal Docks closed in the 1980s, and London City Airport occupies part of the site; Henleys works closed in the 1970s.

To the left on leaving the Ferry is the **London Teleport (32A)** of British Telecom, established 1984, with its truly amazing collection of large and small satellite dish aerials which receive signals from around the world and transmit them through a fibre-optic network.

To the right a pleasant ***riverside promenade (32B)** runs past the remains of North Woolwich pier (which was used by the Great Eastern Railway for the toll ferry from North Woolwich to Woolwich from 1847 to 1908) and **The Royal Pavilion (32C)**, a large pub of 1849, extended 1852, now disused, and into the **Royal Victoria Gardens (32D)** *(see above)*.

The park provides good views of the river and of Woolwich, with St Marys Church prominent and Shooters Hill beyond, Thamesmead to the east and the Thames Barrier to the west. There is also a distant view of some buildings in the Royal Arsenal, in which the mock-Tudor storey of New Laboratory Square stands out.

At the north-west corner of the park is the handsome red brick **Police Station (32E)** of 1904, with a lot of decorative flourishes. In the park, at the south-east corner, is a steam hammer of 1888, which came from the Royal Albert Dock; it was used to shape red hot metal, mainly to form ship girders and ribs.

Beyond the park is a long terrace of 18 houses at **Barge House Road (32F)**, of 1901, the first houses built by the Metropolitan Borough of Woolwich, and a similar terrace of 8 houses at **Woolwich Manorway**. Nearby, on Albert Road, is **The California (32G)**, an attractive pub of 1914 with art nouveau lettering and some architectural oddities.

Opposite the Royal Pavilion pub is ***North Woolwich Old Station (32H)**. The old station is a fine Italianate building of 1854, the front having a recessed upper section behind an unusual balustrade, and two great end pavilions with Doric columns. It is now in use as the Great Eastern Railway Museum *(see below)*, restored and converted to this use in 1984. The new North Woolwich station is alongside.

**Great Eastern Railway Museum.** The museum, which is run by the Passmore Edwards Museums Trust, tells the story of the Great Eastern Railway. The interior has been restored to its condition of c1910, with the staff dressed in Edwardian uniform; the exhibits include a wide variety of steam railway displays and artefacts including train models, equipment, old notices and signs etc.

You enter a large booking hall, with a reconstructed ticket office to the right; the booking hall leads to the vestibule, with the general waiting room to the left and the ladies waiting room (now incorporating a small public library) to the right. Outside is a circular space where a turntable used to be; here is a small shunting tank locomotive of 1876, rebuilt at Stratford 1895. Nearby is a Penfold hexagonal pillar-box c1872. Three of the four original platforms have survived - one is part of the museum (several old carriages are located here), one is still used for the railway service, and one is in the adjoining commercial yard but is now difficult to detect.

> *The museum is open Monday to Thursday and Saturday 1000 to 1700, Sunday & Bank Holidays 1400 to 1700; closed Friday, Xmas Day, Boxing Day. Contact 0171-474 7244. Admission free.*

**33. Waterfront Leisure Centre,** Woolwich High Street. This large and pleasing building was built for the London Borough of Greenwich in 1988; it incorporates magnificent sports facilities, including a 'tropical lagoon style' swimming-pool. It does however form a barrier between the town centre and the river.

**34. The Crown & Cushion**, 37 Woolwich High Street. An Edwardian rebuild of a mid 19th century pub.

**35. *Riverside Walk.** This promenade extends for about half a kilometre from the Foot Tunnel entrance as far as the Royal Arsenal wall, and provides good views of the river and North Woolwich opposite, of the Free Ferry in operation, and of aircraft movements at London City Airport.

The walk is accessible from Glass Yard to the west of the Waterfront Leisure Centre, also at **Bell Water Gate**, and at **Ship and Half Moon Lane,** an alley along the west wall of the Royal Arsenal.

At Bell Water Gate is an old slipway, used as a coal wharf in the 19th century. Nearby is a long wooden pier parallel with the shore, which was used by **Woolwich Power Station**. The first generating station was built here 1895; a large new power station was built 1919-23, and this was demolished in the 1980s - it is now a derelict site **(35A)** awaiting redevelopment. This was the site of the original late Iron Age settlement and of the Roman camp *(see Introduction, page 10)*. In the western part was, according to the most recent research, the site of the shipyard set up by Henry VIII in 1512, the forerunner of the Royal Naval Dockyard *(see 42)*, and the site of the Gun Wharf which replaced it later in the 16th century.

From Ship and Half Moon Lane there are views of some buildings in the Arsenal - the rear of the Royal Laboratory Model Room, and New Laboratory Square (though its mock-Tudor stage is more clearly visible from the riverside walk itself). There is a more interesting view from just round the corner in Warren Lane *(see page 47)*.

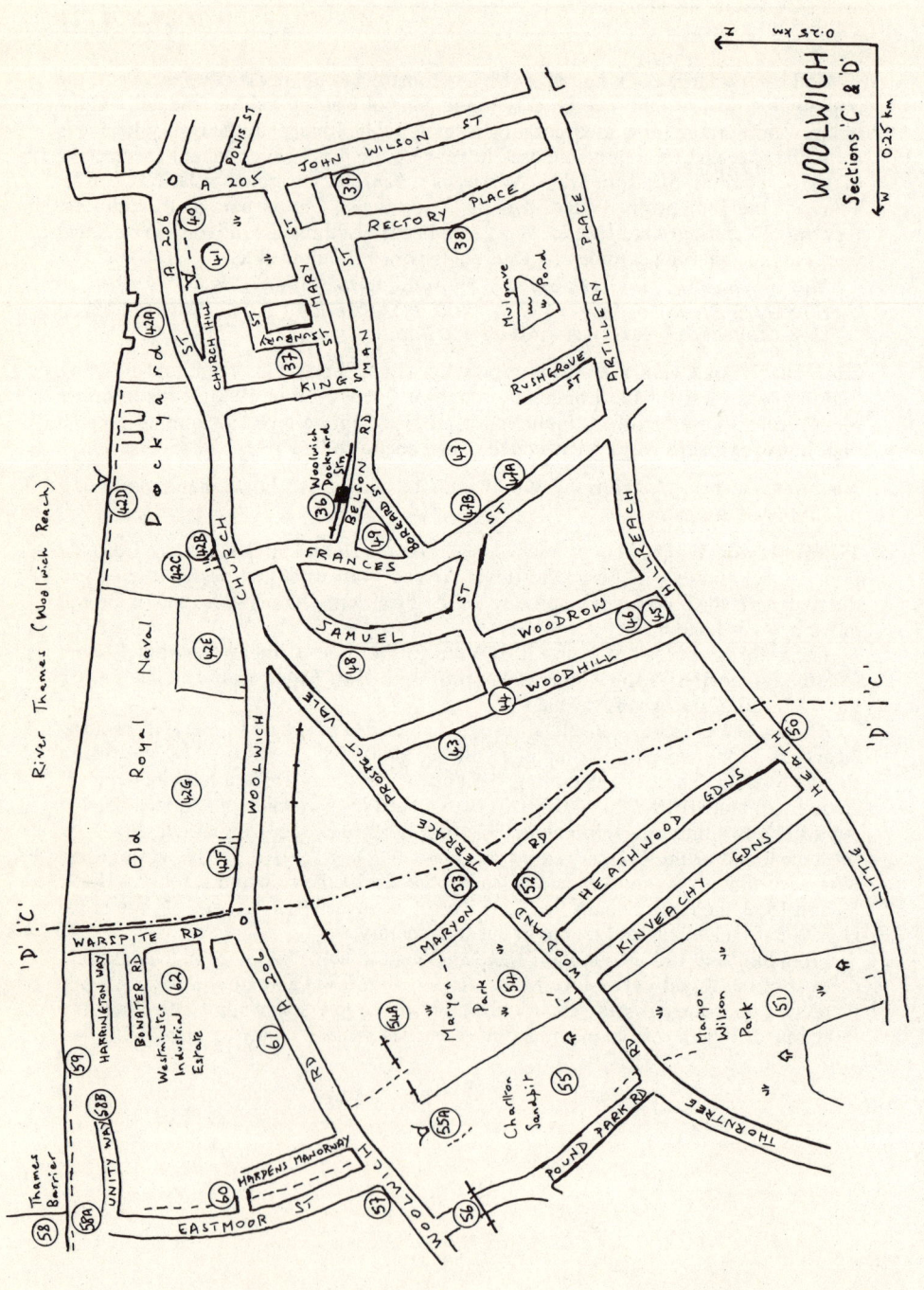

# WOOLWICH

## Gazetteer

### Section 'C' WEST WOOLWICH

**36. Woolwich Dockyard Station** was originally opened in 1849 on part of a former sandpit, known as Bowaters Pits, which extended as far south as the Red Barracks estate. Only the original west wing now remains, a small and basic structure; the main part was not rebuilt after a fire in 1960, the vacant space to the right indicating clearly its site. The platforms with their wooden canopies have quite a dramatic setting in a cutting between tunnels.

**37. Woolwich Fire Station**, Sunbury Street. A quirky building of 1887, distinguished by its prominent circular tower. The upper floor was originally built as flats for firemen.

**38. Woolwich Congregational Church**, Rectory Place. A Victorian Gothic church of 1859, with a tall spire and ogee-shaped entrance archway.

**39. St Marys School.** The original building of 1877 is small and dominated by its shaped gable. A rather similar but larger building was added in 1888. The much larger building to the south was added in 1898.

**40. Coronet Cinema**, John Wilson Street. A cinema of 1937, now the only cinema in Woolwich. The exterior is considered to be the finest surviving example in London of the 1930s 'Odeon' style.

**41. *Church of St Mary Magdalene.** This church, a successor to the original parish church of Woolwich, occupies a commanding position on a hill overlooking the river.

> There is evidence of a church on the hill by c1115, located by the cliff to the west, on the north side of the present footpath; there may well have been a church on the site in the late Saxon period.
>
> The present church, on a site slightly to the south, was built between 1727 and 1739, though the main part had been completed by 1733. It was not, as commonly supposed, one of the '50 new churches' commissioned in 1711; in fact, its application to be treated as such was turned down.

It is a plain Georgian brick church with a square tower, quite handsome with its pedimented entrance at the west end and rows of round-headed first floor windows. The present east end with its Venetian window was added in a sympathetic style by John Oldrid Scott (son of Sir George Gilbert Scott) in 1894. Note the sundial of 1830 on the south wall.

The *interior *(contact the Vestry on the south side, or telephone 0181-316 4338)* is interesting. It now consists of just nave and chancel, as the aisles and galleries above were partitioned off and converted into offices for community organisations in 1961. The impact of the original galleries is inevitably lost, but the nave with its Ionic columns retains a certain elegance. The chancel of 1894 is quite dramatic, in a baroque style and adding considerably to the overall impact of the interior.

In the vestibule is the royal arms of George II. In an office at the west end of the south aisle is a stained glass window commemorating the death of 'Frederick Whomes and 590 others' when the pleasure steamer Princess Alice sank in the Thames off Tripcock Point (now part of Thamesmead) in 1878.

The chancel lies behind a great chancel arch with free-standing Doric columns, and similar arches lead into the organ alcove and the south chapel. The stained glass in the Venetian window is of 1900. In front of the chancel arch is a splendid and finely decorated wooden pulpit of 1897; it is on rails, an unusual feature.

In the south chapel is a finely carved wooden reredos which was at the original 18th century east end. The stained glass over it is of 1909. Also in the chapel are numerous wall monuments, including an ornate cartouche to Daniel Wiseman 1739, and a postwar tablet to the engineer Henry Maudslay who died in 1831 (and was buried in the churchyard - part of his tomb is now in storage in the Royal Arsenal).

The **churchyard** is laid out as a pleasant park; to the north are fine views over the river, including an early part of the Dockyard, and the only remaining monument - to the boxer Tom Cribb 1848, featuring a colossal lion resting its paw on an urn. Some of the park walls are lined with old gravestones.

**42. *Old Royal Naval Dockyard.** The site of the Dockyard now has a variety of uses. It extends for over a kilometre along the Thames, and is still largely surrounded by a high brick wall, partly Victorian and partly postwar.

> The origins of the Royal Naval Dockyard can be traced back to a shipyard set up by Henry VIII in 1512 which began the transformation of Woolwich from a fishing village into an important town. The process accelerated with the establishment further east of The Warren (later to be called the Royal Arsenal), which in the 17th century was associated with the Dockyard, being used for testing guns and for a gun battery.
>
> The shipyard was founded by Henry VIII to build his famous ship 'Henri Grace a Dieu' (or 'The Great Harry'), then the largest ever known. It was completed in 1514, fitted out at the Erith dockyard, and launched in 1515. According to the most recent research, the shipyard was located in the western part of the now derelict Power Station site *(see 35A)*, where the remains of a large Tudor warship were excavated in 1912.
>
> In 1546 a Dockyard was set up to the west below the hill on which the parish church was located. This became the Royal Naval Dockyard, and the original site became a Gun Wharf.
>
> The Dockyard was extended further west during the 17th century; 'The Sovereign of the Seas' was constructed here in 1637. There were further extensions during the 18th century - to the east the Mast Pond was added in 1744, and to the west the area where the surviving Gatehouse and Clockhouse were to be built was incorporated by 1779.

From 1800 the importance of the Dockyard began to decline, though from 1833 and again from 1842 the site was extended westwards for the Steam Factory, the first naval establishment for the manufacture and repair of engines for steamships. However, Chatham Dockyard had been growing fast, and the Woolwich site was found increasingly unsuitable, as the river-bed was silting up and the ironclad boats demanded by the Navy were difficult to launch in the narrow river. The Woolwich Dockyard finally closed in 1869, the same year as the Dockyard at Deptford, the two events causing immense distress throughout the area. Afterwards the site was used for War Department stores.

Recent excavations have revealed building foundations from the 17th to the 19th century; the finds from the excavations are in Greenwich Borough Museum. A number of historical buildings remain, including some late 18th century buildings in the central housing estate section, and some 19th century industrial buildings in the west section where the Steam Factory was located. The larger part of this latter section was acquired in 1926 by the Royal Arsenal Co-operative Society as a warehouse, works and office area and given the name Commonwealth Buildings.

The site now falls into four parts, going from east to west, which was broadly the sequence of historical development:

(i) An industrial area (**42A**), largely derelict, though a section still in use formed part of the Dockyard site of 1546. This area is best seen from St Marys Churchyard. The eastern part, embracing the Ferry car park and the former Cubows shipyard, formed the Mast Pond Wharf of 1744; the western part, which was the Dockyard site of 1546, embraces the Downtown Marine Construction yard, with an old slipway still in use, and an area of waste land, also containing an old slipway (visible as you walk down Church Hill).

(ii) A modern housing estate, now the most interesting section, embracing the 17th and 18th century extensions. This area was developed by the London Borough of Greenwich 1973-80. It is entered opposite Frances Street through a late 18th century gateway, alongside which is the *Gatehouse (**42B**) of the 1780s, an elegant building with Venetian windows and a colonnade, nicely converted to a pub called The Gatehouse.

Ahead is the *Clockhouse (**42C**), formerly the Admiral-Superintendent's Offices, now a community centre. This is a pleasing building of the 1780s, handsome and well-proportioned, with a fine ornamental clock tower. The two wooden porches on either side of the front steps, added in the mid 19th century, are an unusual feature. Inside, note on the ground floor two ceramic tiles showing old cannon, one in the large room to the left and the other in the coffee bar opposite, by W. Lambert 1896; they were brought here c1980 from the demolished Clarence Arms pub in Plumstead. (To the south-west of the Clockhouse is the site of the old Dockyard Church of 1859, which in 1933 was moved bodily to Eltham, and is now St Barnabas Church, Rochester Way.)

At the south-west corner of this area is a pedestrian tunnel under Woolwich Church Street to Prospect Vale. This was formerly a tunnel for a rail siding (opened probably c1860) from the nearby North Kent Line, and still has something of the atmosphere of a railway tunnel. The tunnel into the area further east from Kingsman Parade is modern.

A fine wide *riverside promenade (42D) laid out 1980 runs the length of the housing estate, giving views across Woolwich Reach to Silvertown (where the Tate and Lyle factory of c1930 is dominant), North Woolwich and the Ferry; the Thames Barrier is clearly visible to the west and Canary Wharf and Central London beyond. On the promenade, going from west to east, are: a gun drill battery c1850, with two swivel guns, and the river steps, used for arrivals by water; nearby, a mosaic set into a seat showing the world and the months of the year; a bright ceramic mural portraying a variety of fish; two graving docks of the 1840s used for cleaning the bottom of ships, now filled with water and not very pleasant; near the docks, an old hand winch; and by the river, a mosaic set into the pavement. The mural and the mosaics were the work of a team from the Elfrida Rathbone Society 1984-86.

(iii) A small industrial estate (42E). From the entrance to the estate there is a good view to the west of the surviving buildings of the Steam Factory, especially the chimney and the smithery *(see below)*. On the estate, to the right of the entrance is a mid 19th century timber shed.

(iv) **Commonwealth Buildings**. This vast area, together with the industrial estate *(see above)*, was the site of the Steam Factory. Some 19th century buildings remain near the entrance - to the left the old **apprentices school (42F)**, now the Co-op funeral service; to the right, the old **guardroom** of 1843 and behind, the remaining parts of the main building of the ***Steam Factory (42G)**, built by John Rennie 1842-46. Of this great building, the south range with its row of great round-headed windows was the smithery (built to manufacture metal parts) of 1846, with the brass foundry at the western end, and the north range the marine engine fitting & erecting shop of 1843. By the wall is a 60 metres high factory chimney. Some rail track from the Dockyard sidings is still visible to the north of the steam factory.

The remainder of the area, which extends for nearly half a kilometre along the river, is at present derelict; it will be redeveloped mainly for housing, and will incorporate a riverside walk.

**43. *Woodhill School**, Woodhill. An impressive London School Board school by Edward Robson of 1883, with a striking skyline. The south front is especially impressive, with large distinctively patterned windows, gabled dormers, and corner turrets. The north front is a symmetrical composition and has a quirky turret on top.

**44. Woodhill.** This street retains one early and several mid 19th century houses, some with strongly individual characteristics. Note the following houses, going from north to south - on the east side:

**Nos 129/131**, Elwes Terrace, probably c1845, a tall pair which was part of a group of four houses.

**Nos 143/151**, of the 1840s, nos 143/7 with a series of pilaster strips, and nos 149/151 a large pair with stuccoed ground floor. Next are **nos 153/9**, an attractive though plain terrace, probably c1850.

**Woodhill Court**, 173/5 Woodhill, a tall pair set back in an imposing position, harmonious and quite elegant, probably c1850.

On the west side:

**No 98**, formerly called The Limes, an attractive detached villa, probably of the 1830s, spoiled by pebbledash facing and by the later extensions on both sides. Next are **nos 100/2**, probably c1845, a nice pair with a shared pediment, but with later bay windows.

**Nos 106/110**, probably c1845, a tall and elegant terrace. Directly behind is **Hanging Wood House**, no 112, a large house with a bold porch, also probably c1845.

**Nos 118/120**, probably c1845, a highly attractive pair with a great blank elliptical arch set into the facade. Adjacent are **nos 122/4**, a nice plain brick pair, probably c1850.

**45. Beresford Terrace,** 40/49 Hillreach, probably c1845. An elegant and impressive terrace, a unified composition with regular and distinctive features. Note the fine wrought iron railings leading up to the entrances at first floor level, the paired pilasters along the frontage, the Italianate window-cases on the upper floors, and the rusticated ground floors.

**46. 64 Woodrow.** A handsome house c1860, the original building consisting of the central doorway and the windows on either side, all in round arched recesses. The separate entrance to the right was added and the upper floor windows enlarged in the 1890s when it became the Slazengers tennis ball factory, in which use it remained up to the 1940s. It is still in business use.

**47. Red and Cambridge Barracks.** A pleasantly designed housing estate c1975, small scale and in a vernacular style. It occupies the sites of the former Cambridge Barracks (opened as the Royal Marine Barracks in 1847) to the south and of the former Red Barracks (opened as the Royal Marine Infirmary in 1859) to the north; both became army barracks in 1869. The two surviving original gateways in Frances Street, totally different architecturally, now serve as landmarks leading into the estate.

The *****Cambridge Barracks gateway (47A)** of 1847 is a splendid rusticated stone structure, massive and classical, linked by quadrants with niches to gatehouses with Doric loggias on either side; inside the gateway is a wrought iron lamp holder, and behind are two old cannon.

A short distance to the north is the **Red Barracks gateway (47B)** of 1859, much smaller, of red brick, with lion's heads in the gate piers; the old gatehouse is to the right, and a lengthy stretch of the old wall and railings to the left.

Note that the names of the two mid 19th century pubs opposite, **The Admiral** and **The Navy & Army**, recall the naval origins of the barracks.

**48. Edinburgh Castle,** Samuel Street. A delightful stuccoed pub, its structure basically c1800, but its frontage mid 19th century.

**49. Church of St Michael & All Angels**, Borgard Road. A large and rather raw Victorian Gothic brick church. The chancel is the oldest part, built in 1878 as an extension to an earlier church of 1868; the nave, designed by the famous Gothic Revival architect William Butterfield, replaced the earlier church in 1889. The narrow west aisle was added in 1955. The orientation of the church is to the south. A small part of the original St Michaels Mission School of 1871 remains adjoining the northern end of the church.

The **interior** *(contact 0181-854 2302)* is lofty and impressive, with much elaborate late Victorian decoration. Note the painted wooden vault over the nave, and the extravagant stone and marble reredos of 1892. A First World War memorial crucifix by Sir Ninian Comper faces the entrance at the north end.

# WOOLWICH

## Gazetteer

### Section 'D' THAMES BARRIER & HANGING WOOD
*(See map on page 24)*

*The locations in this section are really part of Charlton; they form the easternmost fringe of Charlton adjoining Woolwich.*

**50. 70 Little Heath.** This small basic house of c1830 in stock brick is conspicuous in this street dominated by red brick houses built between 1890 and 1910. Many of the Edwardian style houses have fine decorative features and form unified groups, a pattern which is repeated in the streets to the north, Heathwood Gardens formed 1897, and Kinveachy Gardens formed 1905.

**51. Maryon Wilson Park.** A small but beautiful park, occupying part of the formerly extensive Hanging Wood. It was opened by the London County Council in 1926.

The park descends steeply from the southern entrance in Charlton Park Road to Thorntree Road in the north. The southern part is quite narrow, with a path running alongside a stream in a valley or 'combe'; the wild plants by the stream include some rare species. Further north, the park is broader, with a central ridge flanked on either side by valleys with streams. There are fine trees and rhododendron bushes. Near Thorntree Road is a children's zoo, with enclosures for deer, sheep and goats.

**52. St Thomas Church**, Woodland Terrace. A stark Victorian Byzantine basilica by Joseph Gwilt of 1850. The exterior is in red and white brick and stone, and has four small corner towers and a striking apse. The nave originally had small circular windows as in the apse, but these were later elongated.

The **interior** is worth seeing *(contact the Rectory next door in Maryon Road, 0181-854 1828)*. In 1982 it was transformed, with a youth centre taking up most of the nave and a newly inserted first floor. The church itself is now quite small, consisting of the apse and a small part of the original nave. The circular windows in the apse have colourful late 19th century stained glass, and there is a font with intriguing patterns and Greek script.

The churchyard has many 19th century and later tombs and gravestones.

**53. 2/28 Woodland Terrace.** An elegant curving convex terrace, probably of the 1840s, made distinctive by its sequence of tall pilaster strips.

**54. \*Maryon Park.** Originally part of Hanging Wood. Quarrying for sand took place here from the early 18th century to 1870. It was opened as a park by the London County Council in 1891.

The grassed area in the centre forms a sort of bowl, surrounded by high ground on most sides. To the north-east is **Cox's Mount (54A)**, with steps leading up from several points to a delightful grassed plateau at the summit.

The main entrance is from the northern end of Maryon Road; there are also access paths from the south - at the western end of Woodland Terrace, involving descent of a flight of steps - and from the north, from Woolwich Road. This latter path is over a railway bridge, with a good view on either side of the tunnels *(see 56)* to the east under Cox's Mount and to the west under the ridge overlooking Charlton Sandpit.

**55. \*Charlton Sandpit**, also known as Gilbert's Pit. This is another disused sandpit (in use from 1870 to 1889), adjoining Maryon Park to the west. It is separated from the Park by a prominent ridge, and is mostly fenced off; access is possible, but it is not easy to find the way in.

> Up to c400 AD there was a substantial Romano-British settlement around the ridge. The settlement was surveyed c1870 by the famous archaeologist Sir Flinders Petrie, who lived in his youth in Maryon Road nearby, and excavated by F. C. Elliston-Erwood 1915; the finds are in Greenwich Borough Museum. Interesting geological formations (lower London tertiaries) are exposed on the side of the ridge, and the area has been designated a 'site of special scientific interest'.

The only access is along a footpath from Thorntree Road which runs behind the houses on the east side of Pound Park Road. The path leads out into the old pit, which is now a grassed bowl similar to Maryon Park. In the far north-east corner another path leads up through the trees to a flight of steps, which leads up to the top of the ridge. From here there is a quite spectacular **\*view (55A)**, embracing the Thames Barrier, the river and East London to the north, and Greenwich and Canary Wharf to the west, with the tall buildings of Central London visible in the distance.

**56. Charlton Lane crossing.** There are not many level crossings left in the built-up area of London. This one is located between Charlton and Woolwich Dockyard Stations, and there is a striking view eastwards of the tunnels under the Charlton Sandpit ridge (141 metres long) and under Cox's Mount in Maryon Park (111 metres long).

**57. The Victoria**, 757 Woolwich Road. A pub of Edwardian appearance, notable for the two large Truman eagles in bas relief on the exterior.

**58. \*\*\*Thames Barrier,** the world's largest movable flood barrier, 520 metres wide, commenced 1972, completed 1982, first used 1983. It was designed for the Greater London Council by Rendel, Palmer & Tritton, and has won awards for its imaginative use of structural steel and concrete. It was an outstanding engineering project, and has become a London landmark.

## 32 - WOOLWICH

*Access by road to the Barrier is best along Eastmoor Street, off Woolwich Road. There is a landscaped walkway from Woolwich Road alongside Eastmoor Street which leads to the Barrier.*

*From the Barrier Gardens Pier to the east there are boat services several times daily (except December to February) to Greenwich Pier, with connections to Central London, and direct to Westminster Pier. There are also summer round-trip cruises lasting approx 25 minutes through and around the Barrier.*

The visible signs of the Barrier are the gleaming shell-like hoods of stainless steel - seven large ones each facing a smaller one - which are perched on massive concrete piers. These piers house yellow rocker beams and hydraulic machinery which can in 10 minutes raise steel gates from a horizontal position on concrete sills on the river-bed to form a barrier over 15 metres above water level.

The gate closest to the south river bank and the three gates closest to the north river bank, ie where the river is relatively shallow, are normally kept in a horizontal position above the water level; these are called drop gates or falling radial gates, whereas the other more central ones (normally kept on the river-bed) are called rising sector gates.

Ships can pass through the four wide gaps between the central piers - note the navigation lights. Prominent on the sides of the piers are the circular gate-arms of steel to which the gates themselves are attached; these gate-arms have wooden strips attached which act as buffers.

One or more of the gates can sometimes be seen in a vertical position for testing purposes, but the full barrier would be in use only when a high surge tide, particularly when accompanied by a strong north wind, posed a flood threat to London. With the rising level of the river and the sinking level of the land around, this threat had over the years become greater. As part of the same Thames flood defence project, the river banks were raised for over 30 kilometres downstream and seven small barriers erected on tributary waterways.

One of the best views of the Barrier is from the terrace of the cafe. There are well laid-out promenades on the south bank on either side of the Barrier, with good views across the river and towards Central London. The promenade goes in a tunnel under the **Control Building (58A)** - note the striking concave roofs of stainless steel, the design of which is reminiscent of the shell hoods of the Barrier itself. The riverside walk continues for a kilometre and a half through the New Charlton Industrial Zone, first to Anchor & Hope Lane and eventually to River Way.

On either side of the Control Building are items of equipment used during the construction of the Barrier, and made into works of sculpture. On the east side are two tremies, or funnels of the pipes used to pour concrete into the pier foundations. On the west side is an anchor and chain used for mooring the concrete sill units.

The **Visitors Centre (58B)** is to the south of the cafe. You first enter a room with a permanent exhibition on the construction of the Barrier, with a working model of a pier and gate, and a video lasting approx 10 minutes; this room then leads to an auditorium where there is a regular 20 minute multi-screen show with stunning sound and visual effects and a rather fulsome commentary.

*The Centre is open daily 1000-1700 (1030-1730 Saturday, Sunday, bank holidays). Admission charge. At the back of the Centre is a shop, though this can be reached separately without paying for admission.*

**Woolwich Arsenal Station (1993)** - *Woolwich 1*

**Royal Arsenal Gatehouse (1829, 1859, 1891)** - *Woolwich 26*

**Town Hall (Sir Alfred Brumwell Thomas 1906)** - *Woolwich 11*

**Gurdwara, Ramgarhia Association (1889)** - *Woolwich 5*

**Church of St Mary Magdalene (1727-33)** - *Woolwich 41*

**Clockhouse, Old Royal Naval Dockyard (1780s)** - *Woolwich 42C*

**Cambridge Barracks gateway (1847)** - *Woolwich 47A*

**Beresford Terrace (c1845)** - *Woolwich 45*

**Thames Barrier (Rendel, Palmer & Tritton 1972-82)** - *Woolwich 58*

**North Woolwich Old Station (1854)** - *Woolwich 32H*

**6/34 Crescent Road (c1849)** - *Woolwich 76*

**219/221 Burrage Road (c1861)** - *Woolwich 82*

**Main Guard House (1788)** - *Royal Arsenal 1*

**Dial Arch Block (possibly Nicholas Hawksmoor 1717-20)** - *Royal Arsenal 4*

**Royal Laboratory Model Room (possibly Nicholas Hawksmoor 1720) -** *Royal Arsenal 6*

**Shell Foundry Gatehouse (David Murray 1856) -** *Royal Arsenal 13*

**Royal Artillery Barracks (1778, James Wyatt 1802)** - *Woolwich Common 2*

**Royal Military Academy (James Wyatt 1806)** - *Woolwich Common 9*

**The Rotunda (John Nash 1820)** - *Woolwich Common 19*

**Mallets Mortar (1854) -**
*Woolwich Common 22*

**The Old Vicarage (1793)** - *Plumstead 12*

**85/91 Genesta Road (Lubetkin & Pilichowski 1935)** - *Plumstead 20*

**The Slade, Plumstead Common -** *Plumstead 13A*

**The Old Mill (mill 1764, pub mid 19th century) -** *Plumstead 26*

**St Nicholas Church (12th century, 1664, 1907)** - *Plumstead 40*

**Plume of Feathers (early 18th, early 19th century)** - *Plumstead 41*

**Severndroog Castle
(Richard Jupp 1784) -**
*Shooters Hill 8*

**Oxleas Wood &
Oxleas Meadows -**
*Shooters Hill 11*

**Water Tower (1910)** - *Shooters Hill 18*

**Christ Church (1856) & Ypres milestone** - *Shooters Hill 2*

**Lesnes Abbey ruins (1178-1200) & Woods -** *Abbey Wood 1*

**Abbey Wood Station (1987) -** *Abbey Wood 3*

In the northern section of the landscaped walkway from Woolwich Road towards the Barrier is a work by the Laotian sculptor Vong Phaophanit, **'Silk and Ash'**, of 1993. It consists of a long glass wall, encasing wood ash on one side and pink silk on the other, with a section cut out and moved back to form a gateway. It has unfortunately been badly vandalised, and is likely to be moved elsewhere.

**59. Foxtrot U475**, a **Russian submarine**. It has been moored to the east of the Barrier since 1994, and was acquired after the break-up of the Soviet Navy. It was built in 1967 near St Petersburg, and was in active service until 1976, but never shot any live ammunition; 22 torpedoes were carried, 2 with nuclear warheads.

> Open daily 1000 to 1800, winter 1000 to dusk, admission charge. Note that several steep stairway ascents and descents are involved, and five low and narrow circular hatches have to be negotiated.

The route through the submarine includes: a narrow corridor lined with a mass of pipes, gauges and valves; the front and rear torpedo rooms; the battery room, the largest room in the submarine; the captain's and commissar's cabins, and officers mess; the galley; the engine rooms. There is no access to the conning tower.

**60. Thames Barrier Arms**, 32 Hardens Manor Way. An attractive mid 19th century pub, formerly known as 'The Lads of the Village'. Its location is isolated, as the housing terraces around have been demolished.

**61. Woolwich College (Charlton Centre)**, a further education college. It was formerly Maryon Park School, a handsome multi-gabled London School Board building of 1896 with twin turrets.

**62. Westminster Industrial Estate.** The estate is an extension of the New Charlton industrial zone; together with the Mellish Industrial Estate, it occupies the site of the AEI-Siemens factory which closed in 1968.

> The Siemens factory was founded here in 1863 for the manufacture of submarine cables; it eventually covered a vast area, expanding into the manufacture of telegraph, telephone and other electrical equipment, and at its peak in 1940 employed over 9000 persons.
> In 1954 Siemens became part of the AEI group, and shortly after the AEI merger with GEC in 1967, a decision was taken to close the factory. This was the first major factory closure in the country since the war; it created a political storm at the time, and heralded a series of other industrial closures in South East London.

Nothing remains of the original Siemens building of 1863, which was in Harrington Way. However, ranges of buildings from 1871 to 1899 remain on the south side of Harrington Way and on the north side of Bowater Road. The oldest remaining building, of 1871, is the building near the end of Bowater Road with a long series of round-headed windows along the ground floor. Most other buildings on the Estate have been built since the closure, though some buildings of the early 20th century remain.

There is no public access to Harrington Way, which belongs to Emafyl, manufacturers of picture frames (their site includes a cluster of recently erected tall silver silos), nor to the raised walkway along the river through the site.

At the end of Warspite Road, **Trinity Stairs** leads down to the river.

# WOOLWICH

## Gazetteer

### Section 'E' BURRAGE TOWN
*(See map on page 14)*

*****Burrage Town**, a residential area consisting mainly of terraces in Italianate and other classical styles, was built between 1840 and 1870. Historically, apart from Brookhill Road and a small section of Sandy Hill Road, it was in the old parish of Plumstead, and is often still considered part of Plumstead. However, as the area is closer to Woolwich Arsenal Station and Powis Street than to Plumstead Station and Plumstead High Street, it is here treated as being part of Woolwich.

The western part of Burrage Town, between Brookhill Road and Burrage Road, has largely survived, and remains an area of great character with attractive groups of houses and some interesting pubs. The most interesting roads are Sandy Hill Road, Crescent Road, Burrage Road, and Conduit Road.

**63. Walpole Arms**, 83 Brookhill Road. A stuccoed pub, probably of the 1850s, with a handsome classical ground floor.

**64. Brookhill Road.** This road was developed from c1844 on the eastern side only, as the western side was in military use. Note, from north to south: nos 71/74, substantial houses probably c1849; nos 42/52, a terrace probably c1844; and nos 2/7, pairs probably c1859.

**65. 27 Willenhall Road**, a large and quixotic late 19th century house with polychrome brick patterns, and quite amazing decoration in the gabled section.

**66. Lord Clyde**, 1 Brookhill Road. A pleasant pub, probably c1859, half hidden below the level of Plumstead Common Road.

**67. Foxhill Centre**, Plumstead Common Road. A pleasant small red brick building of 1881, originally Woolwich High School, with a Dutch gable, octagonal cupola, and much fine ornamental detail.

**68. Fox & Hounds,** 57 Plumstead Common Road. A pub basically c1868, though there has been a pub called Fox & Hounds on this site at least since 1800. Its present appearance is spoiled by modern tile-cladding on the upper floor, added in recent years.

**69. Edge Hill**, in an elevated position overlooking Plumstead Common Road. Developed in the 1860s; some houses have fine ornamental features.

**70. 26/28 Plumstead Common Road**, a pair probably of the 1830s; no 26 is stuccoed and has an ornamental fanlight.

**71. 63/65 Plumstead Common Road**, a brick pair of the 1840s. No 63 is well preserved, no 65 spoiled by later alterations.

**72. Sandy Hill Road.** There were already several houses (including no 110) in Sandy Hill Road before the development of Burrage Town, and it was in fact the first street to be developed as part of Burrage Town, from 1840. Many groups are attractive; note in particular, from south to north:

On the west side, nos 134/144, probably c1843; no 110, a handsome detached house, probably of the 1830s, stuccoed and rusticated, with a portico; Invicta Terrace, nos 90/104, probably c1859; nos 34/60, probably c1842, several with fine decorative features.

On the steep slope from the junction with Crescent Road down to Brookhill Road, Hope Place, nos 9/33, a terrace of 1851 stepped up the hill; and nos 5/7, a large pair probably c1846.

**73. The Melbourne Arms**, 81 Sandy Hill Road. A highly attractive pub, probably of the 1840s, with pedimented upper windows.

**74. Burrage Place** and **Frederick Place.** These developments of the 1850s, despite much alteration, preserve a sense of uniformity on both sides of the road.

**75. Fort Tavern**, 26 Sandy Hill Road. An attractive pub, its present frontage of 1842. It is particularly notable for the interior, with remarkably detailed and intricate wooden carving behind the bar.

**76. Crescent Road.** This road, the most attractive in Burrage Town, was developed from c1847, following a curving route down the hill. There are several pleasing terraces - note in particular, going downhill from south to north: nos 6/34, probably c1849, tall and impressive with pilaster strips; Mars Place, nos 36/40, of 1857; nos 66/86 and St Georges Terrace, nos 65/107, opposite, probably c1854; nos 109/123, probably c1855, with some distinctive decorative features.

**77. 1/17 Conduit Road.** No 1 is a tall detached house, probably c1852, and nos 2/17 form an attractive terrace, probably c1854, with paired entrances under elliptical archways.

**78. Woolwich Polytechnic Upper School.** The original building, of 1876, on Bloomfield Road, is large and severe, but the later building on Sandy Hill Road, of 1890 by Thomas Bailey, is low-lying and has considerable charm.

**79. Duke of Cambridge**, 36 Bloomfield Road. A nice pub of c1856, with Trumans green tiling c1910 on the ground floor.

**80. 71/81 Plumstead Common Road** form a unified sequence of cubic houses, with rusticated and stuccoed ground floors. **Nos 83/89** are two tall pairs with pedimented windows and projecting porches. Both groups are attractive, of the mid 19th century.

**81. Trinity Methodist Church**, Burrage Road. A modern octagonal church of 1969. The design is striking, the support ribs being continued up to form a corona over the building. The interior contains an illuminated stained glass panel of 1994 by Julia St Clair Forde to Stephen Lawrence, victim of a racist murder the previous year. Adjoining to the north is the old church of 1931, now the church hall.

**82. Burrage Road.** This road was developed from c1849, and towards the southern end several good groups of houses have survived. Note in particular, going from south to north:

On the west side, nos 212/226, probably c1862. Opposite, on the east side, nos 193/7, probably c1860, and nos 199/213, probably c1855, many stuccoed; nos 215/217 and (sharing a wide portico) 219/221, probably c1861. On the west side, nos 192/4, probably c1856, and in similar style nos 196/210, probably c1867.

Also note two spiky bargeboarded houses on the east side next to the Methodist church hall, which together with the house in Willenhall Road *(see 65)* are the only Gothic houses in this classical area, no 261, probably c1860, which was the vicarage for St James Church *(see below)*, and no 263, probably c1867, with its tower.

**83. Greenwich Young People's Theatre**, which runs theatre workshops, occupies the former **St James Church**, built as a proprietary chapel for Burrage Town 1855. It is a strange and rather grim building, with tall narrow windows and an open belfry. The interior contains wall tablets to the Pattison family, of Pattisons Pit *(see 1)*; but it is only by climbing the stairs to the old gallery that you get any real impression that this was a church interior.

**84. The Lord Raglan**, 158 Burrage Road. A pleasant pub of c1855. *(See also 22.)*

# WOOLWICH

## Suggested Walks

*It is recommended that the suggested walks be followed in conjunction with the Gazetteer and the maps, and that the Gazetteer be consulted at each location for a detailed description. Most locations described in the Gazetteer are covered; some other locations have not been included, as they might add too much to the length of the walks.*

*Walk no 1 covers Sections 'A' & 'B', Walk no 2 Section 'C', and Walk no 3 Section 'E'. Some external viewpoints of the Royal Arsenal are included towards the end of Walk no 1. The walks follow a more or less circular route, so can be joined at any location. Walks nos 1 & 3 begin and end at Woolwich Arsenal Station, and Walk no 2 at Woolwich Dockyard Station. Section 'D' is not included; the locations are in a logical sequence quite easy to follow, and it is difficult to construct a circular route.*

**WALK no 1** (including General Gordon Place, the Town Hall, Powis Street, the Free Ferry, North Woolwich, the riverside walk, Arsenal viewpoints, Beresford Square). Distance (excluding the Ferry trip to North Woolwich) approx 3 kilometres.

*NB. The Museum in North Woolwich Old Station is closed Friday, Sunday & Bank Holiday mornings. The interior of the Old Granada is a highlight of the walk, so join the bingo club a day beforehand if you can to gain access. Note the access details in the gazetteer for St Peters Church and the Town Hall.*

On leaving **Woolwich Arsenal Station (1)**, proceed straight ahead into **General Gordon Place (3)**. Note **Equitable House (2)** to your right, the **Eauzone (3B)** to your left, and **1/5 Thomas Street** and **Woolwich Post Office (3A)** ahead. Turn left along Wilmount Street to the **Gurdwara (5)**, turn right up Masons Hill and right again into Anglesea Road, passing the **Synagogue (6)** and the **Old Carmel Chapel (7)**. You emerge onto Woolwich New Road by the **Anglesea Arms (8)**. Turn left for the **Church of St Peter (9)**; try to see the interior.

Cross the road into the driveway between Peggy Middleton House and Crown Buildings, then turn left along the footpath, then right to emerge onto Wellington Street by the **Director-General (10)**. Cross the road to the **Town Hall (11)**; ask permission to see the Victoria Hall and (if possible) the Council Chamber. Proceed along **Market Street**, noting **nos 24/28 (12)**, to the end, with **Woolwich Police Station (13)** to the left and the **Magistrates Court** to the right. Turn left up Calderwood Street to the **Gurdwara (14)**.

Return along Calderwood Street until you reach the corner entrance of the **University of Greenwich (17)**. Note in passing the facades of the University along Polytechnic Street and Calderwood Street, and **Miller Freeman House (16)** on the left. Enter the University to see the foyer. Turn right along Thomas Street to the **Earl of Chatham (18)**, then retrace steps.

37

Take the short path opposite the University entrance into **Powis Street (19)**, turn right for **no 12 (19A)**. Return along Powis Street, passing **nos 68/86 (19B)**, **nos 125/161 (22)** and **136/152** (the Co-op buildings), until you reach the **Old Granada (23)** at the end; try to see the interior. Note the **Coronet Cinema (40)**, the old Odeon, opposite.

Proceed straight ahead across the roundabout to Ferry Approach and the **Woolwich Free Ferry (30)**. If you have time, take the ferry to **North Woolwich (32)**, walk along the **riverside promenade (32B)**, and visit the **Royal Victoria Gardens (32D)** and the **Great Eastern Railway Museum** in North Woolwich Old Station **(32H)**. Return on the ferry, or perhaps use the **Woolwich Foot Tunnel (31)**. From Ferry Approach bear left on the north side of Woolwich High Street to the **Waterfront Leisure Centre (33)**.

Note **121/123 Woolwich High Street**, **The Coopers Arms (24)**, and **108/112 Woolwich High Street (25)** opposite. Continue past the Leisure Centre to **The Crown & Cushion (34)**, then bear left down **Bell Water Gate** to the **Riverside Walk (35)**, and turn right alongside the **Woolwich Power Station site (35A)**, so important in Woolwich's history. Ahead is the wall of **The Royal Arsenal**, with the top of **New Laboratory Square** visible. Follow the walk to **Ship & Half Moon Lane**, the bear right until you emerge on Warren Lane.

From here there is a view (though not very satisfactory) of some buildings in the Arsenal. Continue along Warren Lane to Beresford Street, and a section of open railings which gives a good view of some of the historic buildings of the Arsenal. *(See Royal Arsenal, page 47.)*

Cross the main road to the **Royal Arsenal Gatehouse**, and into **Beresford Square (26)**. Note **The Ordnance Arms** and adjoining buildings to the left, and **18/20 Greens End (26A)** ahead. Proceed around The Ordnance Arms into **Woolwich New Road**. Note **nos 1/11 (26B)**, then continue, passing **nos 15/25** and **The Pullman (29)**, and you are back at Woolwich Arsenal Station.

**WALK no 2** (including St Marys Church, the Old Dockyard site, and Woodhill). Distance approx 3 kilometres.

*(NB. It is worth trying to make advance arrangements - see the Gazetteer - to view the interior of St Marys and St Michaels Churches.)*

On leaving **Woolwich Dockyard Station (36)**, turn left along Belson Road, left into Kingsman Street, right into St Mary Street, and left into Sunbury Street. Note **Woolwich Fire Station (37)**, return to St Mary Street and continue to the junction with John Wilson Street. Turn right to **St Marys School (39)**, retrace steps and continue down John Wilson Street to the **Coronet Cinema (40)** and the roundabout.

Bear left up the footpath into St Marys Churchyard, noting the views of the eastern part of the **Old Royal Naval Dockyard (42A)** and across the river. To your left is the **Church of St Mary Magdalene (41)**; try to see the interior. Go down Church Hill and proceed along Woolwich Church Street until you reach the gateway of the Dockyard site opposite Frances Street.

Enter the gateway, passing the **Gatehouse** pub **(42B)**, and go straight ahead to the **Clockhouse (42C)**. Pass to the right of the Clockhouse, then ahead to the **riverside promenade (42D)**, turn right and walk as far as the graving docks. Retrace steps to the Dockyard gateway and turn right along Woolwich Church Street. Continue until you reach the entrance to the industrial estate **(42E)**, from where there is a view of the surviving buildings of the **Steam Factory (42G)**.

Cross the road and go along Prospect Vale, turning left into **Woodhill (44)**. Note **Woodhill School (43)** on the right and nos 129/131 on the left, nos 143/159 on the left, nos 98/102 and 106/112 on the right and Woodhill Court on the left, and nos 108/124 on the right. At the end turn left along Hillreach, passing **Beresford Terrace (45)** and noting **64 Woodrow (46)** near the top of Woodrow, until you reach Frances Street.

Turn left down Frances Street, noting on the right the **Cambridge Barracks gateway (47A)** and the **Red Barracks gateway (47B)**. Turn left along Samuel Street until you reach the **Edinburgh Castle (48)**, then retrace steps to Frances Street and turn left. Turn right down Borgard Street along the old wall of the Red Barracks to the **Church of St Michael (49)**; try to see the interior. Continue to Woolwich Dockyard Station.

**WALK no 3** (covering Burrage Town). Distance approx 4 kilometres.
On leaving **Woolwich Arsenal Station (1),** turn left along Woolwich New Road, left into Anglesea Road and immediately turn sharp right up Brookhill Road. After reaching the **Walpole Arms (63)**, look left up Sandy Hill Road **(72)** to see **Hope Place** on the left, but continue ahead along **Brookhill Road (64)**.

At the end climb the steps to the **Lord Clyde (66)**, and continue up Plumstead Common Road, passing the **Foxhill Centre (67)**, until you reach **Fox & Hounds (68)** and the crossroads. Note **Edge Hill (69)** and **26/28 Plumstead Common Road (70)** opposite, and turn left down **Sandy Hill Road (72)**. Note in particular on the left nos 134/144, no 110, and nos 90/104; on the right the later **Woolwich Polytechnic Upper School building (78)** and **The Melbourne Arms (73)**; and on the left nos 34/60 and **Fort Tavern (75)**.

Bear right down **Crescent Road (76)**; note in particular on the left nos 6/40 and 66/86, and on the right nos 65/123. Turn right up Bloomfield Road, passing the original **Woolwich Polytechnic Upper School** building **(78)** on the right and the **Duke of Cambridge (79)** on the left, and at the top turn left. Note **71/89 Plumstead Common Road (80)**, turn left into **Burrage Road (82)**; note **Trinity Methodist Church (81)** opposite, try to see the interior.

Proceed along Burrage Road; note in particular on the right nos 261/263 and nos 193/221, and on the left nos 212/226 and nos 192/210, then on the right **Greenwich Young Peoples Theatre (83)** and on the left **The Lord Raglan (84)**. Turn left along Raglan Road and cross into **Conduit Road (77)**, noting nos 1/17 on the left. Cross into Anglesea Road and continue to the end, then turn right along Woolwich New Road to return to Woolwich Arsenal Station.

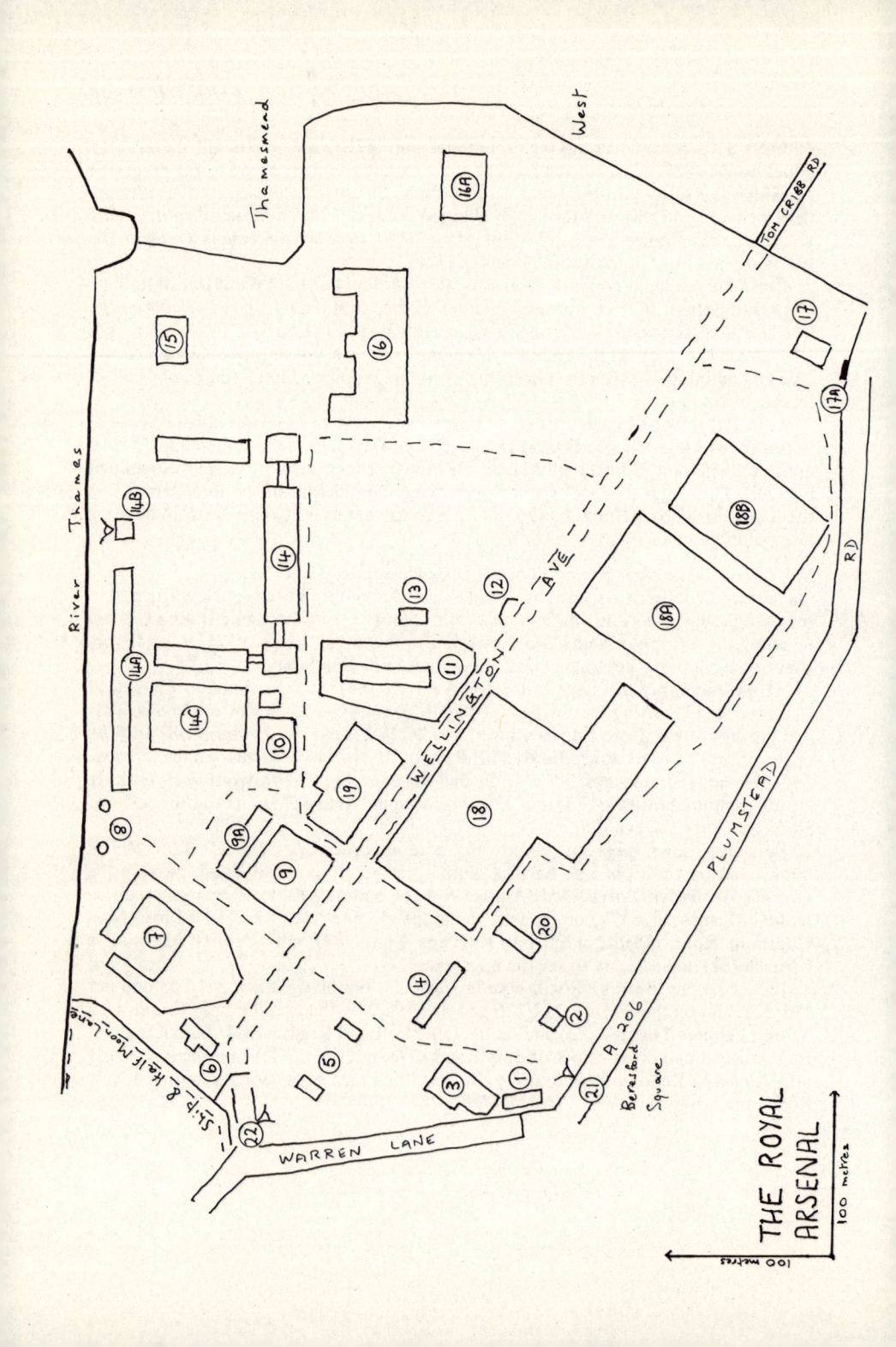

# THE ROYAL ARSENAL

# THE ROYAL ARSENAL

## Gazetteer

\*\*\***The Royal Arsenal.** This was the oldest and greatest arms factory in the country, as well as the original home of the Royal Artillery and the Royal Military Academy. The site was finally vacated at the end of 1994; though no longer a security area, there is as yet no regular public access. *(For viewpoints and access, see pages 46-47.)*

The site contains one of the most important collections of industrial buildings of the 18th and 19th centuries in the country. Their preservation, and ready public access to them, are of outstanding national importance.

The present site occupies only a small proportion of its former size, which by the end of the 19th century extended eastwards for about five kilometres to the Crossness Sewage Works. But it is still large, extending half a kilometre along the river and a similar distance inland. On the landward side it is surrounded by a high brick wall, parts of which date back to 1804.

>The site of the Royal Arsenal was originally called Woolwich Warren. A shipyard which was the forerunner of the Royal Naval Dockyard had been set up to the west along the riverside in 1512, and a gun wharf in 1546. In the 17th century the Warren became an ancillary area for the Dockyard; it was used for testing guns, and a gun battery was located there. In 1671 the Crown purchased a Tudor mansion there called Tower Place, and used its grounds as an ordnance storage depot, replacing the gun wharf; it soon became the largest gun repository in the country.
>
>The development of the Warren as an arms factory began in 1696, when the Royal Laboratory was built; of this great building, two blocks have survived. In 1716, following a disastrous accident at a privately owned foundry at Moorfields in the City of London, it was decided to build the first Royal Brass Foundry at the Warren *(see also Woolwich Common 19)*. Also in 1716 the Royal Regiment of Artillery was founded at Tower Place, the barracks being located around Dial Square from 1719; the regiment remained there until 1778. In 1720 an Academy was set up in a new building on the site of Tower Place, which later became the Royal Laboratory Model Room; this became the Royal Military Academy in 1741, remaining there until 1806.
>
>The Warren had been renamed The Royal Arsenal by George III in 1805, and it continued to expand throughout the 19th century, particularly during the Napoleonic Wars and around the time of the Crimean War.
>
>It was to become by far the largest arms factory in the country, employing over 80,000 persons at its peak during the first world war. The site at that time was vast, embracing the Plumstead Marshes, with many parts connected by two railway systems, standard gauge (dating from c1850, and linked to the main line) and narrow gauge (dating from 1873).
>
>In 1940 over 30,000 persons worked there, but employment declined as wartime bombing led to much activity being moved away. After 1960 activity was run down drastically; in 1967 the Royal Ordnance Factory closed, and (apart from a small area) the eastern part of the site was released to be incorporated in Thamesmead. The western part of the site continued in use for Quality Assurance until the end of 1994, when the Royal Arsenal finally closed.

41

*In the second half of the 19th century a conducted tour of the Arsenal was a favourite tourist attraction. During that period the Arsenal comprised four departments, occupying broadly separate parts of the site. The official route for visitors went to each department in turn - the Royal Laboratory Department in the west, the Grand Store in the north, the Royal Gun Factories in the east, and the Royal Carriage Department in the south. The sequence of locations in the gazetteer follows very broadly this route through the site.*

**1. \*Main Guard House.** This building of 1788 has a fine pedimented portico of four Doric columns facing inwards to the site.

**2. \*Verbruggens House**, a fine Georgian house which is now, because buildings around have in recent years been demolished, in a rather isolated location. It was built in 1773 for the joint master founders, Jan & Pieter Verbruggen.

**3. \*\*\*Royal Brass Foundry.** This building of 1717, the finest in the Arsenal, is a remarkable and well-preserved early industrial building. Although basically stock brick, the vividness of its abundant red brick dressings almost makes it appear a red brick building. Its design has traditionally been attributed to Sir John Vanbrugh, but this is now considered doubtful.

The main block is elegant and impressive, with its great entrance archway topped by a royal arms, and above the fanlight, the arms of the Duke of Marlborough. The handsome roof is surmounted by an ornamental lantern. The one-storey wings on either side with their separate roofs and round-headed windows add harmony and dignity to the frontage. The only major alterations have been in 1774, when a rectangular block to the south was reconstructed and the lantern clad in lead, and c1878, when the west side was extended. The building was well restored in the 1970s, and is now used as storage for the National Maritime Museum.

The plan of the building is reminiscent of a Georgian church, with a vestibule leading into a nave with aisles on either side. This can best be appreciated in the **interior**, which has exposed roof timbers.

The furnaces for the founding of brass cannon were set up in the taller parts of each aisle and in the rectangular block to the south, and molten brass was poured into pits in the nave floor. Guns were cast here until c1870. The wing to the west of the entrance was a workshop housing clay for model making, and the wing to the east the drawing office and patent room.

Outside the building to the east is a badly eroded stone figure with the inscription: 'Deus Lunus, late Roman work, brought from Egypt'.

**4. \*Dial Arch Block.** Only the entrance front with its powerful archway remains of the former gun machining factory built 1717-20, which with other buildings covered a wide area and was originally known as the Great Pile. The design has traditionally been attributed to Sir John Vanbrugh, but it is now considered that it may have been designed by Nicholas Hawksmoor.

Guns cast in the Brass Foundry were bored and machined here. The archway has massive piers topped by cannon balls (added in the 1980s), and is flanked by low wings with steep roofs and end gables. The sundial over the entrance is of 1764. The cast iron inner arch is of 1780. Some late 19th century cast iron columns, which once supported the roof of the building behind, are set into the north side of the block. In the square beyond some lengthy sections of track of the narrow gauge railway have survived.

**5. *Royal Laboratory.** Two separate and similar pavilions of 1696 are all that remain of the Laboratory, which was a vast ammunition factory. They are the oldest buildings on the site. They were in fact built as the entrance blocks of two long ranges (demolished in the 1960s and 1970s) which faced each other across an open courtyard. The courtyard was roofed over in 1854 to form the largest covered factory shopfloor then known; the level of this roof can be detected on the two pavilions.

Both pavilions are at present derelict, and the eastern one, which is in particularly poor condition, has lost its original roof. But the elegant design of the frontispieces facing inwards to the courtyard is clear. The frontispiece of the western pavilion, with the arms of William III in a pediment, is better preserved.

**6. **Royal Laboratory Model Room.** A highly distinctive and dramatic dark brown brick building, built 1720 on the site of (and probably using the foundations of) the 16th century mansion of Tower Place. The design has been traditionally attributed to Sir John Vanbrugh, but it is now considered that it may have been designed by Nicholas Hawksmoor.

A powerful frontispiece is flanked by sides with tall round-headed windows and circular windows above; the northern end has a large bow. The detail of the frontispiece is worth studying - note the heavy rusticated piers of the porch, the tall recessed upper arch flanked by narrow windows with oval windows above, and the clock of 1836 and the wind direction indicator at the top; the lion and unicorn on pedestals above the porch were formerly over a gateway of the Royal Laboratory.

The large room to the right was originally the Board Room of the Board of Ordnance, and the large room to the left the Academy; this became the Royal Military Academy in 1741, and at that time the extension to the rear of the building may have been added. After the Academy had moved to its new building on Woolwich Common in 1806, the building became the Model or Pattern Room for the Royal Laboratory.

Attached to the rear wall is a gauge which was used in testing explosive charges.

The *interior is worth viewing. The room to the left has an an early wall painting depicting trophies, though the top has been cut off by an inserted floor. The room to the right retains its original impressive dimensions; it has a great stone early 18th century fireplace, and an elegant apse-like bow.

**7. *New Laboratory Square.** Between the Royal Laboratory and the river is this large complex, consisting of four long blocks around a courtyard. The west range is of 1805, and the east range with its central pediment c1810; both are impressive, and largely as originally built. The north range is c1810, but has a prominent and rather incongruous mock-Tudor top storey, added probably c1920. The south range is of 1878, extended c1890, but its present external appearance is of the 1920s.

The courtyard can be entered at the north-west corner and through a passage in the east range; both east and west ranges are pedimented, and it looks quite impressive overall. Some cast iron columns have survived on both sides of the south range.

**8. *Riverside Guard Houses.** These two small octagonal buildings of 1815 (perhaps designed by James Wyatt or his nephew Lewis Wyatt) originally guarded the riverside entrance, which was an important access to the Arsenal. The river is now blocked from view by flood defence walls erected in the 1970s. The eastern building has lost its original conical roof.

The western building has a plaque commemorating its use in 1879 as a temporary mortuary chapel for the French Prince Imperial, son of Napoleon III, who had been killed while serving with the British Army in South Africa.

Note outside the eastern building an old point lever for the standard gauge railway.

**9. Paper Cartridge Factory**, also known as the Cap Factory. An imposing classical building of 1856, though much altered.

Adjoining at the rear and facing north is the ***Royal Laboratory Offices (9A)**. The central section, with its stone porch and pediment, and two bays on either side formed the original building of 1856. With its long later 19th century extensions on both sides, the building presents a fine classical frontage. The interior has an elegant staircase of 1856.

**10. *Chemical Laboratory.** This classical building is particularly attractive. The recessed central section and the three bays slightly projecting on either side formed the original building of 1864; the extension to the east is of c1885. A glance through the windows on the west side shows a large room with an elegant gallery extending the full height of the building; this was the room used for chemical experiments.

The adjacent building in similar architectural style was the **Naval Offices**. It was built in 1890, the upper storey added in 1903.

**11. Central Offices.** This is a large and heavy neo-Georgian building of 1903-11. The main entrance, with the royal cypher of Edward VII above, is of 1908. Through an archway to the north, which has the royal arms above, can be seen a steel framed lattice bridge across the courtyard.

Until recently there was a magnificent **stained glass window** depicting 'Edward III inspecting his artillery', possibly late 16th century and copied from an older tapestry, in the fanlight over the main entrance. It is known to have been in the fanlight of the Royal Brass Foundry in 1750, but its earlier history is unknown. It has been removed and is now in storage on the site.

**12. *Wellington Memorial.** The marble statue of the Duke of Wellington was sculpted by Thomas Milnes in 1848, and was originally in the Tower of London. It was brought to the Arsenal in 1863. It is now the central feature of a memorial area set up in 1974, incorporating ironwork of 1854 from the Royal Laboratory.

**13. *Shell Foundry Gatehouse.** Only the entrance block of the Shell Foundry, built by David Murray in 1856, survives; it is baroque and impressive, with great arches and paired columns, Doric below and Ionic above. The rest of the massive building was demolished in 1967.

The magnificent cast iron gates to the central archway and side windows were designed by Charles Bailey and cast at Regents Canal Iron Works in 1856, and are amazingly elaborate and intricate. They were removed to the Royal Ordnance Factory at Patricroft, Manchester, in 1968, but were returned to the Shell Foundry in 1991.

**14. *Grand Store.** The centrepiece of this monumental classical composition, built 1806-13 and traditionally attributed to James Wyatt and his nephew Lewis Wyatt, was originally a grand quadrangle open to the Thames. Though derelict in part, the original buildings of the grand quadrangle have remained largely unaltered and are among the most important surviving warehouses of the period in the country. However, the erection in front of a number of large later buildings makes it difficult to appreciate the impact it once had.

The Grand Store consists of west, south and east ranges, and great corner pavilions. The long south range is particularly fine. Rusticated archways link the ranges and the pavilions, though the archway linking the east range to the east pavilion is no longer there.

Blocking much of the view towards the river is a long **shipping shed (14A)** of 1860, partly rebuilt c1890. A similar shed to the east has been demolished, though part was converted c1970 to form a **viewing platform (14B)** after the flood defence walls had been constructed; the views across and along the river are magnificent, and from here can be seen two jetties (originally of 1872, reconstructed 1922) now in an undeveloped part of Thamesmead. Within the quadrangle are three storehouses c1890.

The grand quadrangle was originally flanked by two smaller quadrangles, also built 1806-13. The only building to survive from these, the **Shot and Shell Store (14C)**, was within the western court. It was substantially altered in 1856, c1890, and again in 1972, and only the lower storeys of the north and south ranges survive from the original building. It incorporates a prominent brick tower, built as a water tower c1890 and part of the Arsenal hydraulic system.

Much of this massive complex is now used for storage by the British Library.

**15. The Boiler House**, with its prominent chimney and two oil tanks, is of 1968. It occupies part of the site of the eastern court of the Grand Store. Some small sections of track of both the narrow and standard gauge railways have survived on waste land to the south.

**16. *Armstrong Gun Factory**. A handsome building by David Murray of 1856, in an Italianate style. It has a long E-shaped front facing north, and fine polychrome brick detail. The main range (apart from the front porch) was raised in height in 1911. The iron plates along the north front were to strengthen the internal structure; the building was essentially a frame for six gantry frames, supported on substantial iron piers. The extension to the south is of 1968. The building is now used as storage for the British Library.

It was the focal building of a complex which comprised the Royal Gun Factories. The only other building to survive from this complex is the iron-framed **Rolling Mill (16A)** to the east; it was built c1868, and clad in green corrugated iron in 1890 and later. Other buildings in the complex were demolished in the 1970s.

Several small sections of standard gauge railway track have survived on the waste land to the south of these buildings.

17. *__Middle Gate House__, an attractive building with a Doric porch, now enclosed. It was originally the Storekeepers House, of 1809. The large extension to the rear was added in 1938.

In front is __Middle Gate (17A)__, with four vermiculated gate piers of 1843. It was formerly known as Plumstead Gate, and is now blocked.

18. *__Royal Carriage Factory.__ This massive building, where gun carriages were manufactured, was built 1802-05, replacing an 18th century building. The outer ranges have survived with relatively little alteration, except for extensions at the south-east corner in the late 19th century. However, the core of the building, a massive workshop covered by a corrugated sheet, is modern - it was rebuilt in 1937 and again in 1968. The north front with its corner pavilions, arches, pedimented centre and cupola (with a clock of 1806) is particularly impressive. All sides except the east retain grand entrance archways.

To the east are two large buildings built for the Royal Carriage Factory - first the __Completing Shop, Forgers Shop and Turnery (18A)__, c1860; and beyond the __Timber Shed (18B)__, of 1857. The grand long west range of the Timber Shed with its corbelled cornice remains relatively unaltered and impressive, otherwise these buildings have been substantially altered in the late 19th century and in this century.

Further east, beyond this complex of buildings, note the testing ramps for tanks, constructed 1970.

19. *__Mounting Shed.__ A long and attractive one-storey building of 1887, with a great series of round-headed windows. Guns were mounted on their carriages here; the entrance was purposely located opposite an entrance (now bricked up) to the Royal Carriage Factory. A section of standard gauge rail track enters the building from the north. The interior is impressive, and retains its original iron gantries for overhead travelling cranes. This is the most complete surviving industrial building on the site.

20. *__Officers Quarters.__ A tall and plain brick building, with porches at either end. It was originally built in 1718, and some of the fabric of that building may remain; but it was substantially rebuilt during the 19th century, probably c1850.

This building is visible over the fence from behind Verbruggens House; but the only access is by going behind the Royal Carriage Factory.

There are a number of survivals from the Royal Arsenal which are outside the present site. The most important are: the Royal Arsenal Gatehouse, or Beresford Gate, now cut off from the main site by Plumstead Road (*see Woolwich 26*); part of the old Arsenal canal, now known as Broadwater, in Thamesmead West; and eight 'tumps' or moated magazines of c1890, in Thamesmead Central and Thamesmead North.

> *Since the Ministry of Defence vacated the site at the end of 1994, the question of public access to the site has been in a transitional stage, and it is not yet certain when, and even if, ready public access will become available. At present the site is controlled by the agents Hillier Parker; for those with a special interest, it may be worth contacting the agents on 0171-629 7666 to request a special authorisation to visit the site. Open days and conducted tours are occasionally organised, and it may be worth contacting the Woolwich Town Centre Development Agency on 0181-312 5251 to check whether such an event is being organised. The sole access at present for both pedestrians and vehicles is off the northern end of Warren Lane.*

Plans are under way to convert the western part of the site, where the most important historical buildings are located, into a museum area. The Royal Artillery Heritage Museum plan to move into the Royal Laboratory Model Room and New Laboratory Square. The Greenwich Borough Museum and the Greenwich Local History Library plan to move into Verbruggens House, Dial Square Block, the Main Guard House (where pedestrian access into the site will be reinstated), and probably the Royal Brass Foundry. These plans should come into effect by 1998. It does not however follow that there will be ready public access to other parts of the site, where other important buildings are located.

An area in the eastern part of the site will be occupied until 1998 by the Royal Artillery, and there is no public access at all to this area, which includes Middle Gate House and the two large buildings to the east of the Royal Carriage Factory.

In the meantime, unless authorisation to visit the site is obtained, the public has to make do with views from outside. At present there is one major and some minor viewpoints which afford satisfactory views of some of the more important buildings, though less satisfactory views of others. It is particularly frustrating that the views of the two most important buildings, the Royal Brass Foundry and the Royal Laboratory Model Room, are not very good. Other important buildings can be seen only in part, or are hidden from view altogether.

The major viewpoint (21) is a section of open railings in Plumstead Road, behind the Royal Arsenal Gatehouse in Beresford Square, which looks onto Dial Arch Square, a green surrounded by fine buildings. A tree-lined avenue leads from this viewpoint towards the old riverside entrance. To the left is a good view of the Main Guard House with its portico, and beyond a disappointing view of the side only of the Royal Brass Foundry, though the Roman 'deus lunus' figure can be seen. Ahead is a good view of Dial Arch Block, and to the right, of Verbruggens House. Further away, to the left the east block of the Royal Laboratory can be seen; and to the right the Officers Quarters and the rear of the Royal Carriage Factory are clearly visible in winter.

Other viewpoints which afford glimpses of important buildings are as follows:

A section of open fencing (22) in Warren Lane by the entrance gives, to the left, a disappointing view of the rear and side only of the Royal Laboratory Model Room; ahead, a view of the Paper Cartridge Factory and Mounting Shed, and of the side of the Royal Carriage Factory with the cupola of the north front visible; to the right, a view of both blocks of the Royal Laboratory and of the rear of Dial Arch Block, and a distant view of the Royal Brass Foundry.

Middle Gate House is visible over the wall at Middle Gate in Plumstead Road.

The building visible over the wall from the Riverside Walk is the New Laboratory Square (west and north ranges).

It is also worth noting that the promenade in front of the Royal Victoria Gardens in North Woolwich *(see Woolwich 32B)* gives a distant view of some buildings near the river. On the right is the north range of the New Laboratory Square, with its mock-Tudor top storey. In the middle can be seen the two small riverside guard houses, one without its original roof, and the brick tower of the Shot and Shell Store. On the left, the east range of the Grand Store is visible, but the rest is hidden from view by shipping sheds and other later buildings.

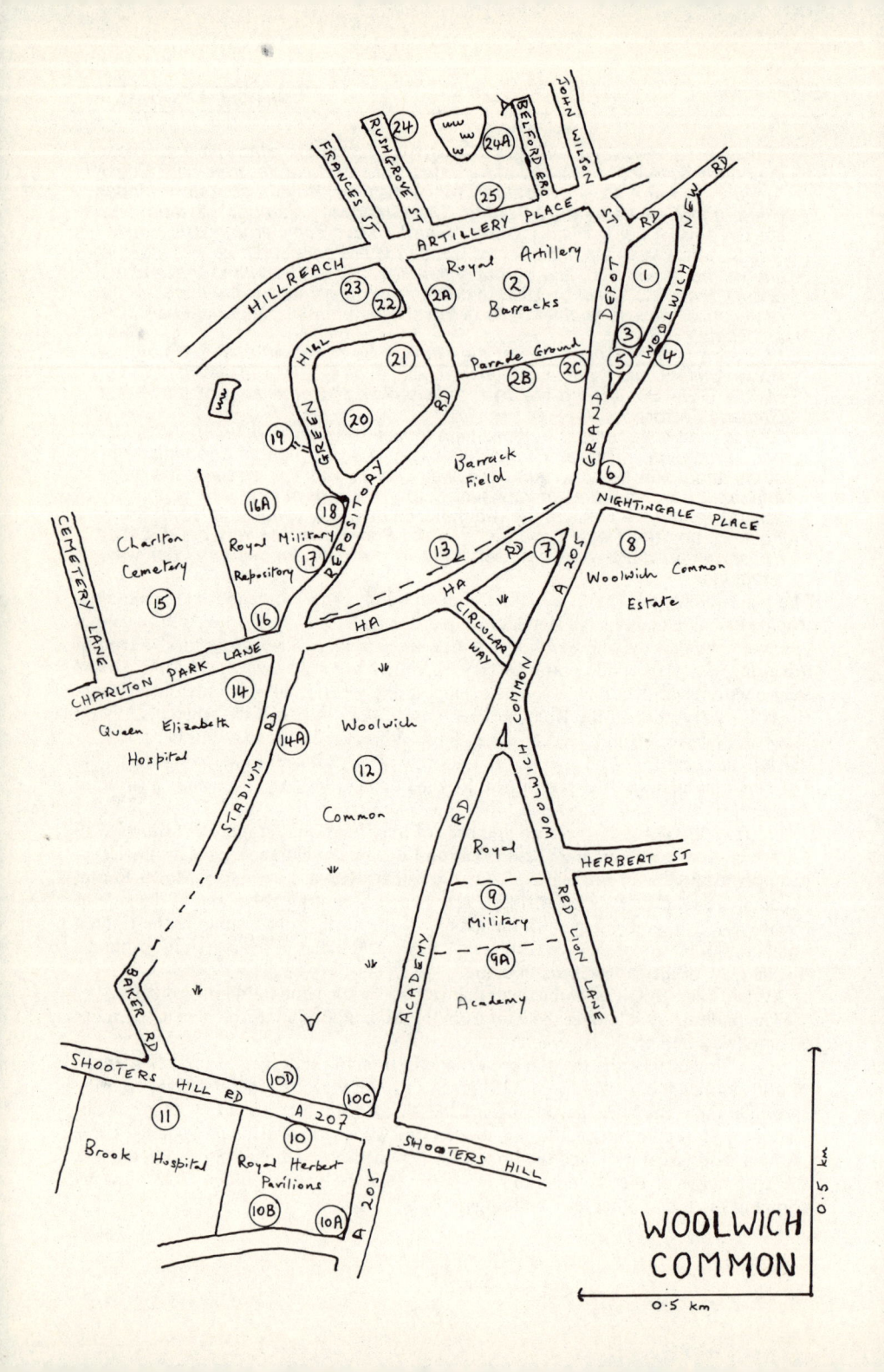

# WOOLWICH COMMON

# WOOLWICH COMMON

## Gazetteer

**1. *Connaught Mews.** The three buildings are of 1780 and originally formed the Royal Artillery Hospital, the first military hospital in the country; they became the Connaught Barracks after the Royal Herbert Hospital opened in 1865. A large extension to the north of 1806 has been demolished. The whole site is surrounded by a brick wall which is in part the original wall of 1806.

The three original buildings were converted handsomely by Parkview Properties for a housing development called Connaught Mews c1992. They are visible from the former entrance in Grand Depot Road; the entrance is now in Woolwich New Road. A fine early 19th century wrought-iron lamp-holder which was over the original entrance has been preserved inside as a feature on the green in front of the central building. The site of the 1806 extension to the north has recently become a new housing estate.

**2. ***Royal Artillery Barracks.** The south front of the Barracks is a magnificent Georgian facade 330 metres long, dominating Woolwich Common and the southern approach to Woolwich. The east half was built in 1778 and the west half with the arch to join them together added by James Wyatt in 1802. It is the longest continuous architectural composition in London, and 'can be compared only to St Petersburg' (Pevsner).

> The Royal Regiment of Artillery was founded by Colonel Albert Borgard at Tower Place in The Warren (which became The Royal Arsenal) in 1716. *(See also Royal Arsenal, page 41).* The site was later found too restricted, and the Board of Ordnance purchased from Richard Bowater (of Bowaters Pits) farmland facing Woolwich Common for construction of a new barracks in 1776. More space was needed for drill and practice, and in 1802-06 the Board purchased full rights to the use of Woolwich Common. The expansion of the Artillery led to increased military enclosure of parts of the Common. By 1810 the Royal Artillery area on the Common consisted of the Barracks, the Barrack Field in front, and to the west the Gun Park and the training and storage area known as the Royal Military Repository. Since then many other buildings forming part of the Artillery Garrison have been erected on and around the Common.

In the centre is an ornate white triumphal arch, surmounted by trophies and a lion and unicorn; on either side of the arch are three brick ranges linked by gleaming white stuccoed colonnades of four Doric columns supporting a balustraded balcony. The facade is totally symmetrical, except for a colonnade in the western half which projects a short distance; this was in fact moved outwards as late as 1921.

The projecting colonnade is the Palm Court, or entrance lobby, of the *Officers Mess, which occupies a series of magnificent reception rooms. The Palm Court leads into the Hall, with the Mess Room, the most splendid room, on the left; a staircase leads up to the Music Room.

## 50 - WOOLWICH COMMON

The Mess Room was part of the building of 1802, but it was extended to its present shape and appearance in 1843. The central chandelier is thought to be from the Prince Regent's palace in Pall Mall, Carlton House, which was demolished in 1829. In a niche at the end is 'Armed Science', a statue by John Bell 1855.

To the right of the Hall is the Silver Room, built in 1967 for permanent display of the mess silver. It is an extraordinary collection, and includes: a candelabrum in the form of a palm tree, presented by William IV 1833, the largest and most conspicuous item; an Abyssinian cross, 14th or 15th century; a gold ram's head, from West Africa; the Empress Eugenie shield of 1858, presented by Eugenie, consort of Napoleon III.

The Mess Room, Hall and Music Room contain a large collection of paintings, principally portraits (many being copies) of monarchs and artillery commandants. Probably the most important is a portrait by George Frederick Watts of General Sabine 1874, in the Hall.

Apart from the Officers Mess, the barracks behind the facade were largely rebuilt 1958-68. The main entrance is to the west, and nearby is an **ancient stone (2A)** from Luneburg Heath, Germany, where Germany surrendered on 7th May 1945.

In front of the facade, across the Parade Ground, are a number of guns and monuments. In the centre is the **Crimean War victory memorial (2B)** by John Bell 1860. Also note the heavy granite memorial 1904 to General Sir Alexander Dickson, Master Gunner and Artillery Commandant in the early 19th century, and his son. On either side of this memorial are two Chinese bronze guns, probably 17th century; from the cascabel (the button at the breech end) of these guns Victoria Crosses have been cast since their inception at the time of the Crimean War. Other guns along the Parade Ground include Florentine and other mid 18th century Italian guns, two Russian mortars of 1801, and at the west end a finely decorated Indian bronze gun of 1775.

But the most interesting gun is at the east end, by Grand Depot Road - the *****Bhurtpore Gun (2C)**, a brass gun cast for Emperor Aurangzeb of India in 1677 and captured at the siege of Bhurtpore in 1826. It rests on a massive gun carriage which was constructed in the Arsenal 1828 for presenting the gun to George IV; it features elephants, panthers, a lion, palm trees and zodiac wheels.

In Grand Depot Road, opposite the barracks, is the sole surviving example in the Woolwich area of the **K2 type of red cast-iron telephone kiosk**, designed by Sir Giles Gilbert Scott in 1927. This type is distinguishable from the later K6 *(see 16)* in that all panes of glass are the same size.

> *The public are no longer permitted to walk alongside the Parade Ground between Grand Depot Road and Repository Road. This walk gave a wonderful view of the Barracks, as well as of the guns and monuments on the way. Now the public is restricted to the views from the roads at either end of the Parade Ground. The views of the Barracks are still good, of the guns and monuments rather less so. In particular, only one side of the Bhurtpore Gun and its carriage can be seen, and there is only a distant view of the Victory Memorial. It is to be hoped that at some stage the public will once again be allowed to walk alongside the Parade Ground.*
>
> *The Officers Mess is not open for visits by individuals. For those with a serious interest, it may be possible to join a special party visiting the Mess, and it may be worth writing to the President, Mess Committee, Royal Artillery Barracks, to ask whether such a visit is being organised.*

3. **\*Royal Garrison Church of St George (ruin).** The garrison church was built as a polychrome Victorian romanesque basilica by Thomas Wyatt (a cousin of James Wyatt) in 1863. It was bombed in 1944 and is now a striking and impressive ruin. It is preserved as a memorial garden, and is occasionally used for open air services; the interior is not normally open to the public, but there is a good view from the porch. (The present garrison church is the old Royal Military Academy chapel, *see 9A* .)

The ruin consists basically of a strong Lombard porch with two side porches, all with elaborate columns; and a strong east end with an apse covered with tiled patterns and a coloured mosaic of St George. There was much lavish and extraordinary decoration, and amongst the surviving features, note the angel-head and foliated capitals on the porch columns; the startling peacock and phoenix mosaics flanking the apse; the stone pulpit attached to the chancel arch columns; colourful mosaics of vines and birds in the two side chapels; and the sundial on a plinth in the nave.

4. **\*Engineer House**, accessible by a flight of steps from Woolwich New Road. An elegant Georgian house of 1803, with a beautiful fanlight. Formerly the office of the Royal Engineers, it is now a community centre for military families.

5. **Boer War memorial**, a red granite obelisk of 1902.

6. **Government House.** An early 19th century building, with a strong enclosed porch and a canted bay to the north. The top storey was added later, and there have been large modern extensions. It is now an office building of the Artillery Garrison.

7. **The Little Memorial**, to Rob John Little, a marines officer who died in 1861. Originally a drinking fountain, now there is just a grey granite obelisk. Note, among the biblical inscriptions: 'Solomon saith: wine is a mocker, strong drink is racing, and whosoever is deceived thereby is not wise - Proverbs 20'. Nearby is a late 19th century drinking trough.

8. **Woolwich Common Estate.** The jagged, restless and tiered frontage of this large estate built 1968-82 overlooks Woolwich Common and Nightingale Place; the estate is a complex incorporating several architectural styles. The tall block, **Nightingale Heights**, is of c1969, but was attractively restored and refurbished in 1994, with an elegantly curved roof which is the boiler house for a new central heating system. The tiered terraces facing west and north are of 1980-82, and further east, **Long Walk**, of 1979. Long Walk includes a long terrace stepped up to a tall tower as it climbs the hillside, and incorporates a winding pedestrian walkway at an upper level.

9. **\*\*Royal Military Academy.** The old Academy buildings form a large battlemented complex in Tudor style overlooking Woolwich Common. The imposing 220 metres long north front was built by James Wyatt in 1806.

> The Royal Military Academy was founded in 1741 in the building in the Royal Arsenal which became the Royal Laboratory Model Room. The need for more space led to the construction from 1805 of this large new building for the Academy on the opposite side of Woolwich Common from the Artillery Barracks. In 1945 it transferred to Sandhurst to merge with the Academy there, and the complex (though only partly in use) is now in the control of the Artillery Garrison.

The centre block, of stock brick, has four octagonal corner turrets and ogee shaped cupolas; the ground floor windows are Tudor and the upper floor windows Gothic. This block is linked by stuccoed arcades to two stock brick ranges of the same period, which are in turn linked by arcades to red brick end pavilions, which with the red brick side ranges were added in 1862. The heavily battlemented red brick lodges are of 1877.

The complex in part preserves its original railings. There are three splendid entrance gates, two on Academy Road on the west side and one (ornamented with gilt crockets) at the foot of Red Lion Lane on the east side. Many of the buildings preserve beautiful original projecting lamp-holders.

In front of the centre block are several old guns, including two Dutch guns of 1614 and 1630 with very fine decoration, two 17th century Chinese guns, a cannon of 1719, a late 18th century French gun, and a British cannon of 1812. In the arcades on either side are a number of old mortars - French and Italian 17th century mortars and Russian mortars of c1800. At the very front of the parade ground are more modern guns, including some Russian guns captured during the Gulf War. In a courtyard to the rear of the centre block is an unusual Penfold hexagonal pillar box c1872.

The rear of the complex has another range, with two large archways, of the original building of 1806, flanked by ranges of 1862. Opposite is the plain red brick **Academy Chapel (9A)** of 1902, with a splendid stained glass west window by Christopher Whall 1920; in 1945 it became the Royal Garrison Church of St Michael & All Angels. On the ground in front is a great stone first world war memorial laid by the Woolwich & District branch of the Old Contemptibles Association.

The centre block houses the Royal Artillery Museum on the upper floor, and the library of the Royal Artillery Institution on the ground floor. The library is open to the public only by special appointment. The Museum, covering the history and the campaigns of the Royal Artillery Regiment from its founding in 1716 to the present day, closed to the public in 1995.

*With the closure of the Museum, there is no longer any public access to the complex; however, there are good views of the buildings from outside. It is planned to open a new Museum of Artillery, including this collection and the collection in the Rotunda, within the Royal Arsenal site (occupying the Royal Laboratory Model Room and New Laboratory Square) by 1998. It is probable that the guns now in the complex will also be moved to the new Museum.*

**10. *Royal Herbert Pavilions,** Shooters Hill Road. The old Royal Herbert Hospital is in the course of a superb conversion by Parkview Properties to a housing estate. It is a dramatic but very heavy building complex with a classical frontage. Note the massive stone piers with ornamental lamp-holders on either side of the frontage, linked by quadrant railings to the main building. The hospital was built by Sir Douglas Galton in 1865 as the general hospital of the Artillery Garrison at Woolwich.

> The design of the Royal Herbert Hospital was in its day considered pioneering, with wards in separate pavilions leading off long corridors. Galton was a nephew of Florence Nightingale, and she probably had a great influence on the design on her return at the end of the Crimean War. It was closed in 1978, when the Queen Elizabeth Military Hospital on Woolwich Common was opened.

The large block fronting the main road, with a great round central arch in the middle of the rusticated entrance block, is the old administration building. Behind and on either side are seven two-storey pavilions at right angles; all the pavilions are linked on both floors by a corridor 230 metres long. In the central pavilion, a grand staircase leads to a large chapel on the first floor.

In the grounds are two buildings c1865, both now converted for housing - **The Lodge (10A)**, formerly known as Herbert House, on Well Hall Road, and **259 Broad Walk (10B)**, originally the mortuary.

Opposite the complex are the **Victoria Day Centre (10C)**, formerly the Medical Officers Mess of 1909, an attractive curved red brick building with terracotta ornamentation; and **Adair House (10D)**, formerly nurses quarters of 1928, in severe classical style.

**11. Brook Hospital.** A large hospital of 1894-96, built as an infectious diseases hospital alongside the old Royal Herbert Hospital. The hospital closed at the end of 1995, and the future use of the site is uncertain.

The vast complex contains a number of imposing original buildings and structures, which hopefully will be retained in any future use. These include the Dutch-gabled **porters lodge**; behind, two gabled buildings with similar decorative features - the larger building to the left was the **administration block** and the smaller building to the right the former **doctors quarters**; the prominent **water tower** and front boundary wall, built of red brick with black brick patterns; and, towards the rear of the complex, two ranges of handsome red brick retaining wall with rounded bastions.

The ragstone building by the Shooters Hill Road entrance, vividly contrasting with the predominantly red brick of the remainder, was originally a **pumping station** of the Kent Waterworks Co of 1863, though this use ceased after a new pumping station in Well Hall Road opened in 1922. In the wall by the entrance is a late Victorian **wall letter-box**.

**12. Woolwich Common.** The remaining part of a much larger common, which merged into the now disappeared Charlton Common. There is complete public access, although it has been under Army jurisdiction since being sold to the Board of Ordnance in 1802-06.

The north part, which is sometimes used for fairs and circuses, looks rather desolate. The south part is wild and somehow remote, with rough grass, scrubland and thorn thickets, and there are extensive views from the higher parts.

**13. *Ha-Ha**, or boundary ditch. The north side of the ha-ha is brick the whole length of 600 metres (excepting breaks for road access). Originally constructed between 1777 and 1804, it separates the Barrack Field from Woolwich Common.

**14. Queen Elizabeth Hospital.** This attractive modern complex, consisting of linked low-lying white blocks designed by the celebrated partnership of Powell & Moya, replaced the Royal Herbert Hospital as a military hospital in 1978. It came into National Health Service use at the end of 1995. The entrance is across a low bridge over an ornamental pool with fountains on either side. The staff accommodation and a social club are in separate blocks to the south.

**Woolwich Stadium (14A)** occupied a site opposite the Hospital from 1920 to c1975. The outline of the stadium can be readily detected.

**15. Charlton Cemetery**, Cemetery Lane, laid out in 1855. It has no landscape interest, but there are some interesting memorials. There are two contemporary Gothic chapels.

## 54 - WOOLWICH COMMON

To the right of the entrance is a canopy over an effigy of Jemima Ayley 1860. In front is the memorial to General Orde Wingate of the 'Chindits', killed during the Burma campaign 1944.

To the left of the entrance is a tomb within a railed enclosure to Samuel Phillips 1893, founder of Johnson & Phillips, manufacturers of submarine cables at Victoria Way, Charlton, with bust and the inscription 'Write me as one who loved his fellow men' *(see also Shooters Hill 3)*.

In the east part the most prominent tomb is to Thomas Murphy 1932, owner of the former Charlton greyhound track, with three conspicuous columns and two greyhounds.

**16. Repository Gatehouse.** A building of c1806 with a fine classical pedimented portico, converted to a private house. Outside are the old 19th century gateposts of the Royal Military Repository, now flanking the beginning of Repository Road.

The **Royal Military Repository (16A)** was set up in 1779. The grounds extending north to Hillreach were enclosed in 1805-06, and much of the present wall between Repository Road and Maryon Road survives from that time.

In the northern part of the area is the Repository Wood, containing dense woodland (a remaining part of the ancient Hanging Wood) and a large lake. The southern part contains a handsome Edwardian building which was originally the Army Medical Stores; a group of large late 19th century storage buildings; and one building, basically mid 19th century though much altered, with a series of exterior iron columns used to support the roof of adjoining buildings since demolished. The future of all these buildings on the site is uncertain.

> There is absolutely no public access to the southern part of the site. However, there is a view, though not always satisfactory, of the buildings from outside. The northern part of the site is at present closed to the public, but it is possible that the lake and woodland area may be opened to the public in the future.

In Charlton Park Lane, to the south of the Gatehouse, is the sole surviving example in the Woolwich area of the **K6 type of red cast-iron telephone kiosk**, designed by Sir Giles Gilbert Scott in 1935. This type is distinguishable from the earlier K2 *(see 2)* by its narrow rectangular panes of glass.

**17. Afghan & Zulu Wars memorial,** by Count Victor Gleichen 1881. A monument of rough-hewn rock with copper trophies of both Afghan and Zulu arms.

**18. Railway gun.** This large howitzer is the sole survivor of five such guns made in 1917-19; it is mounted on a proof carriage of 1886, on a section of railway track. These guns were the largest pieces of ordnance ever to enter British land service. Railway-mounted guns were still in use for coastal defence in the last war.

**19. \*\*The Rotunda.** An extraordinary building, which started life as the central tent amongst six erected by the famous Regency architect John Nash at Carlton House Gardens in 1814 for a premature celebration of victory over Napoleon. It was transferred to this site to become the Museum of Artillery in 1820, and for this purpose John Nash added an elegant concave tent-shaped lead roof to protect the canvas, placed it on a brick surround, and installed a massive central pillar. In a 1975 restoration the original canvas and lead roof were replaced.

The **Museum of Artillery** provides a complete exhibition of the history of the gun from 1320 onwards. Basically the museum is divided into six sections, laid out clockwise - I 14th century wrought iron ordnance; II cast iron ordnance 1450-1850; III early rifled ordnance 1850-85; IV early breech-loaders 1885-1902; V first world war ordnance; VI second world war ordnance. In an annexe at the far end facing the entrance are Sections VII machine-guns 1865-1918 and VIII small arms 1500-1939. The number of exhibits is vast; most are well labelled, though they are not always in the section one might expect, and it is sometimes difficult to understand where one section ends and another begins.

Amongst the many exhibits the following are particularly noteworthy, going clockwise. In Section I, a bombard, a 'peterara' (a swivel gun) and a 'serpent' gun, all of the 15th century; and a gun and carriage recovered from the wreck of the Mary Rose, which sank off Spithead 1545. In Section II, a 'galloper' of 1685 to which a horse could be harnessed, a small brass howitzer of 1782, and General Congreve's 'perpetual motion' clock. At the entrance to the annexe, an American Gatling machine gun with ten Colt barrels 1865; in the annexe is an example of Maxim's automatic 'Pom Pom' machine gun of 1903 made in the Vickers works at Erith. In the area around the central pillar are a number of trophy guns, gun carriages used at the funerals of British sovereigns from Queen Victoria onwards, a French field gun presented to Queen Victoria by Napoleon III 1858, and a French triple bore gun captured at Malplaquet 1709. In the last section very near the entrance are a fantastic multi-coloured Burmese bronze gun in the form of a dragon, captured at Mandalay 1885, on an ornamental carriage made in the Arsenal 1858; and alongside an extraordinary Indian mortar in the shape of a squatting tiger, probably late 18th century, captured at Kurnaul 1839.

Just outside the entrance to the grounds is a guided missile launcher of 1958. Just inside the gates, on either side of the path, are two British brass howitzers, one of 1760 and one of 1814. In the grounds are many more guns, including an extraordinary small 15th century Chinese gun; 16th century guns from Malta and Egypt; 17th century guns from Britain, India, China, Portugal and Denmark; later guns from many countries, etc, etc. In a prominent position immediately opposite the museum entrance is a fine large Saxon gun of 1733.

Amongst the display of guns by the far fence opposite the entrance is the spoiled casting of the famous Moorfields gun; following an explosion (causing 17 deaths) when molten metal was being poured into the mould during recasting of this French gun at a private foundry at Moorfields in the City of London in 1716, the decision was made to establish a government arms foundry at Woolwich *(see Royal Arsenal 3)*. Also in this area is a section of the Iraqi 'super-gun' c1990.

The grounds also contain a large number of exhibits of this century, including field guns, anti-aircraft guns, tanks, radar, and a light aircraft. There are also some Russian guns captured during the Gulf War 1991.

*The Museum is open weekdays only 1300 to 1600; closed weekends and public holidays. Admission free. It is planned to open a new Museum of Artillery, including this collection and the collection in the Royal Military Academy, within the Royal Arsenal site (occupying the Royal Laboratory Model Room and New Laboratory Square) by 1998. It is probable hat the guns now positioned on the Common near the Rotunda and those in the Royal Military Academy complex will be moved to the new Museum.*

## 56 - WOOLWICH COMMON

**20. Royal Artillery Observatory.** A simple pedimented building built by the Royal Artillery Institution c1840, used as an observatory till 1926. It was then extensively altered in conversion to a small barracks, and is now in office use.

Nearby are two cannon of 1859 in a defensive emplacement, and two large coast guns of 1896 and 1902. A third gun, the one nearest to the Observatory building, is an example of the **Woolwich Infant** which was manufactured at the Arsenal in great numbers between 1870 and 1910; it was brought from Gibraltar in 1995.

**21. Gun Park Block.** A handsome mid 19th century building, now part of a complex with later buildings. The Gun Park was used for storing guns and for gun practice.

The six stone blocks to the south were until c1990 used for a group of mortars which are now in the arcades of the Royal Military Academy *(see 9)*. Up to 1860 a mortar battery was positioned here for practice on the Common.

**22. *Mallets Mortar.** One of a pair of mortars, the largest ever made. Weighing 42 tonnes, they were designed by Robert Mallet and constructed in the Arsenal in 1854. The mortars could fire a shell a kilometre and a half, but they were never used in war; 91 cm shells made for the mortar are in front. The other Mallets Mortar was until recently in the Royal Arsenal site, but has now been moved to Fort Nelson, Portsmouth.

**23. *Greenhill Courts.** A large and imposing Georgian style complex built 1851-55, which was originally the school for children of the Artillery Garrison. It is now privately owned and was superbly converted for residential use by Parkview Properties in 1989.

The complex consists of four large corner blocks, connected by lower ranges. The north range with its central pediment was the main entrance. Two enclosed squares, entered through doorways in the east and west ranges, are attractive features. The west square retains the iron framework of a former courtyard building.

**24. Rushgrove House**, Rushgrove Street. A building of 1815, enlarged in 1839, and extended to the north in 1855. It was formerly the Artillery Commandant's house. The building is now privately owned, and is difficult to see behind the high brick wall. To the right are stables and coach-house, much altered, and behind these a small octagonal garden house, which is not visible from the road; these outbuildings belonged to an earlier house, and may be late 18th century.

To the east of the house is a large lake, called **Mulgrave Pond (24A)**, which provided water to the Artillery Garrison and to the Royal Arsenal. There is a view, in winter, from Belford Grove of the garden front of the house and of the lake. The lake can be accessed, but only at times when it is used by a local angling club, by following a footpath from Rectory Place north of the grounds of Mulgrave School to a gate in the wall; this provides the only view of the garden house from any point to which there is any public access, but even then it is unsatisfactory, being obscured by the wall and fences.

**25. Army House**, 45 Artillery Place. A small but attractive pub, probably basically mid 19th century, with Trumans green tiling c1910 on the ground floor.

# WOOLWICH COMMON

## Suggested Walk

*It is recommended that the suggested walk be followed in conjunction with the Gazetteer and the map, and that the Gazetteer be consulted at each location for a detailed description. Most locations described in the Gazetteer are covered; some other locations have not been included, as they might add too much to the length of the walks. The walk follows a more or less circular route, so can be joined at any location; it begins and ends at Woolwich Arsenal Station. Distance approx 5 kilometres.*
*NB. The Museum in the Rotunda is only open weekdays 1300 to 1600.*

On leaving Woolwich Arsenal Station, turn left up Woolwich New Road, passing General Gordon Place and the Church of St Peter. Bear right up Grand Depot Road, noting **Connaught Mews (1)** through a gate on the left. A little further and you will have a good view of the **Royal Artillery Barracks (2)**; there is also a view of the **Bhurtpore Gun (2C)** and a distant view of the **Crimean War Victory Memorial (2B)**. Continue up Grand Depot Road, passing the **Garrison Church ruin (3)**, **Engineer House (4)** (which can be seen by walking along the far side of the church ruin), and the **Boer War Memorial (5)**, until you reach the road junction. On the left is **Government House (6)**, and on the right the **Little Memorial (7)**.

Continue alongside **Woolwich Common (12)**, noting the **Woolwich Common Estate (8)** and Nightingale Heights on the left, until you get a good view of the **Royal Military Academy (9)**. Return across the Common, or use Circular Way, and proceed ahead to Ha Ha Road and the **Ha-Ha (13)**, then bear left along Ha Ha Road to the junction. Ahead is the **Repository Gatehouse (16)** and across the road on the left **Queen Elizabeth Hospital (14)**.

Turn right along Repository Road, noting on the left the **Afghan & Zulu Wars Memorial (17)** and the **railway gun (18)**. Turn left into Green Hill, and take the path on the left to **The Rotunda (19)**; if possible, visit the Museum inside. Retrace steps to Repository Road and turn left. Note on the left the **Artillery Observatory (20)** and the guns outside, and further along, **Gun Park Block (21)**. You now have another good view of the **Royal Artllery Barracks**. Continue along Repository Road, noting on the right the **ancient stone (2A)**, and on the left **Mallets Mortar (22)** and **Greenhill Courts (23)**.

At the road junction, turn right along Artillery Place and cross the road. Go down Rushgrove Street for **Rushgrove House (24)**, though the view is rather unsatisfactory. Continue along Artillery Place, passing the **Army House (25)**, and if it is winter, go down Belford Grove for the view of the rear of Rushgrove House and of **Mulgrave Pond (24A)**. Continue down Artillery Place and Wellington Street, passing the Town Hall, until you return to General Gordon Place and Woolwich Arsenal Station.

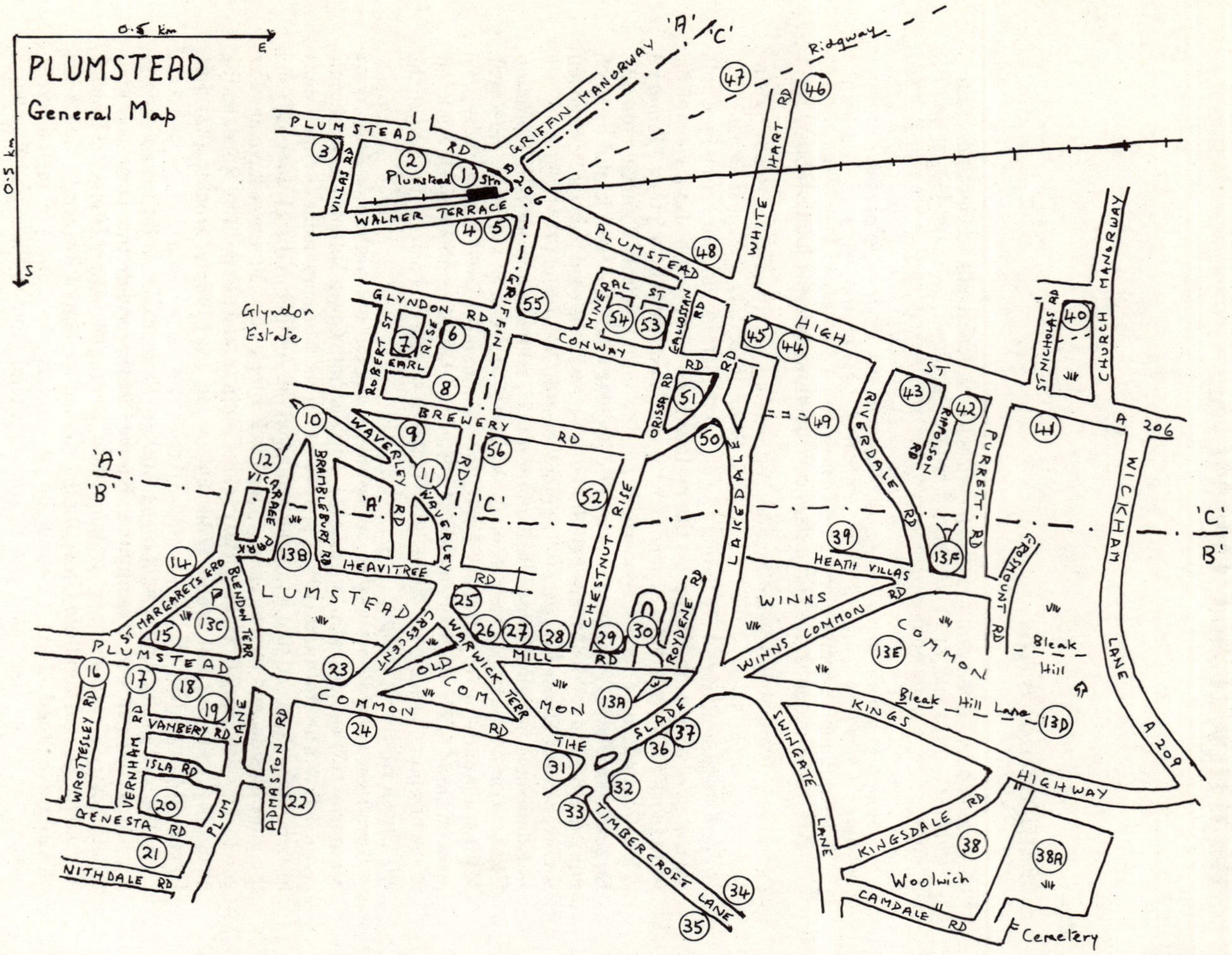
PLUMSTEAD
General Map
0·5 km
E
S
Plumstead Stn
PLUMSTEAD RD
VILLAS RD
WALMER TERRACE
A206
GRIFFIN MANORWAY
'A' 'C'
Ridgway
WHITE HART RD
PLUMSTEAD
HIGH ST
GLYNDON RD
Glyndon Estate
ROBERT ST
EARL RISE
GRIFFIN RD.
MINERAL ST
GALLOSSAN RD
CONWAY RD
BREWERY RD
ORISSA RD
WAVERLEY
WAVERLEY RD
VICARAGE PARK
BRAMBLEBURY RD
HEAVITREE RD
CHESTNUT RISE
LAKEDALE RD
RIVERDALE RD
RIPPOLSON RD
PURRETT RD
ST NICHOLAS RD
CHURCH MANORWAY
WICKHAM LANE A 209
A 206
'A' 'B'
'C' 'B'
HEATH VILLAS RD
WINNS COMMON
WINNS COMMON RD
CROSMOUNT RD
Bleak Hill
Bleak Hill Lane
LUMSTEAD COMMON
ST MARGARETS RD
BLENDON TERR
PLUMSTEAD COMMON RD
CRESCENT
WARWICK TERR
OLD COM
MILL RD
ROYDENE RD
THE SLADE
KINGS HIGHWAY
SWINGATE LANE
KINGSDALE RD
Woolwich
CAMDALE RD
Cemetery
TIMBERCROFT LANE
WROTTESLEY RD
VERNHAM RD
VANBERY RD
ISLA RD
LANE
PLUM
GENESTA RD
NITHDALE RD
ADMASTON RD
1 2 3 4 5 6 7 8 9 10 11 12 13A 13B 13C 13D 13E 13F 14 15 16 17 18 19 20 21 22 23 24 25 26 27 28 29 30 31 32 33 34 35 36 37 38 38A 39 40 41 42 43 44 45 46 47 48 49 50 51 52 53 54 55 56

# PLUMSTEAD

## Introduction

Plumstead could be considered virtually a suburb of Woolwich - the two areas merge between Burrage Town and Griffin Road. But the main part of Plumstead has two clear zones, each of which have a distinct character and identity - the area around Plumstead High Street and the old church, and the plateau to the south formed by Plumstead Common.

Plumstead lost its contact with the river when the Plumstead Marshes, a vast area between the Southern Outfall Sewer embankment and the river, were absorbed by the late 19th century expansion of the Royal Arsenal. This area has now become part of Thamesmead, and it is interesting to note that Thamesmead West is in fact much closer to Plumstead than to the centre of Thamesmead.

### Early history

A Bronze Age burial mound has survived, and Roman remains have been excavated *(see Introduction to Woolwich, page 10)*. There was a Saxon settlement in Plumstead at least by c960. The first stone church, basically the south aisle of the present church of St Nicholas, was built in the 12th century on a patch of firm ground jutting out into the marshland; the river bank at high tide was considerably closer than now.

In the medieval period there was a small village to the south of the church, and a few smallholders in the marshes. At that time Plumstead was probably more populous than Woolwich. To the south orchards stretched up the steep slopes to the Common, and dense woodland stretched beyond up to Shooters Hill.

### The growth of housing

The earliest surviving groups of houses are of the 1840s and are located around the south-west edge of Plumstead Common.

The whole area remained relatively rural until after the mid 19th century, when housing developed rapidly with the expansion of employment at the Royal Arsenal for the Crimean War. The opening of the railway station in 1859 added to the momentum. Housing spread on both sides of the High Street, round the irregular edges of the Common, and in the hilly streets linking the two areas.

By the end of the century Plumstead was largely built up, and its housing remains predominantly late Victorian and Edwardian. There has been some postwar housing by the Borough Council, but the only really large development has been the Glyndon Estate, built 1959-1981 between Plumstead Station and Burrage Town.

# PLUMSTEAD

## Gazetteer

### Section 'A' WEST PLUMSTEAD
*(See map on page 58)*

**1. Plumstead Station.** Originally opened in 1859, and still substantially the original building. Steps lead down to a footbridge over the platforms with their wooden canopies, located in a deep cutting.

Cross to the north side of the main road for an interesting view from Plumstead Bridge of old sidings. To the north of the main line is a yard still in use with several tracks, from which one track continued until c1960 as the 'marsh siding' to the Royal Arsenal extensions on the marshes. Also north of the main line, note the small section of track going back west, which went into the Arsenal site to connect with the Arsenal standard gauge railway; it opened 1876, and closed after 1960. To the south of the main line is a siding which used to run eastwards into the Royal Arsenal Co-operative Society coal depot at Reidhaven Road.

**2. Woolwich Mosque**, still in course of construction, due for completion 1996. It is of red brick, with many round-headed windows; the dome and minaret have yet to be added.

**3. Woolwich College (Plumstead Centre)**, a further education college, a plain modernist building with bands of concrete, purple brick and glass, of 1967.

Adjacent, to the west, is **The Dover Castle**, 91 Plumstead Road, a pleasant pub, probably basically of the 1840s.

**4. Plumstead Radical Club**, 83 Walmer Terrace, has an attractive classical facade of 1902, with decorative details picked out in green.

**5. The Lord Derby**, 89 Walmer Terrace. An impressive pub, originally c1860. It was reconstructed in 1938, though retaining its previous ornate appearance. It is battlemented on top, as are several nearby shops along Plumstead High Street.

**6. The Prince Rupert**, 40 Glyndon Road. This pub in the middle of the Glyndon Estate, originally called Park Estate Tavern, is probably c1870. It was in part radically altered when reconstructed in 1939, but still retains its original Italianate appearance.

**7. St Johns Church**, Earl Rise. A low-lying church, built 1960 in Gothic style, though quite different in appearance from the original Victorian Gothic church of 1884 destroyed during the war.

**8. South Rise School**, Brewery Road. The original multi-gabled London School Board building of 1875 looks imposing amongst the numerous postwar buildings in the grounds.

**9. Brewery Road Chapel.** This chapel, now derelict, was built for the Peculiar People in 1882.

**10. The Rose Inn**, 2 Waverley Road. A handsome pub of c1862; the adjoining terrace, **4/8 Waverley Road**, is also c1862 in similar Italianate style. Next is **10 Waverley Road**, also c1862, a detached villa with a strong doorcase; and then the old wall of the **Kent Waterworks Co**, which was first opened in 1854.

**11. 19 Waverley Crescent.** A Gothic chapel of 1885, now disused. It was first the Union Baptist Church until c1907, then the Peculiar Peoples Chapel until c1934, then Plumstead Particular Strict Baptist Chapel until 1954.

**12. \*The Old Vicarage**, Vicarage Park. Formerly known as Bramblebury, this is a large and very handsome Georgian house of 1793, with a particularly elegant fanlight. The one-storey extensions are original, as are the twisted railings. Between 1859 and 1966 it was the vicarage of St Margarets Church (demolished 1970).

# PLUMSTEAD

## Gazetteer

### Section 'B' PLUMSTEAD COMMON
*(See map on page 58)*

**13.** *****Plumstead Common**, incorporating **Winns Common** to the east beyond Lakedale Road. This plateau hangs on the northern slopes of Shooters Hill and overlooks the High Street area and Plumstead Marshes. It is unexpectedly varied and extensive, two kilometres in length, but quite narrow in places and criss-crossed by roads. To the south several late 19th century terraces form a hard edge to the Common.

> Plumstead Common originally belonged to Queens College, Oxford, though the parish council had grazing rights and free access. In the early 19th century the College began to enclose certain areas; from 1871 onwards the college allowed the Army access to the land, and large areas were turned into a military training ground with no public access. In 1876 John de Morgan of the Commons Protection League led a procession from Beresford Square to remove the fencing; the protest which followed has become known as the 'Plumstead Common riots'. John de Morgan was imprisoned, and further protest led to his release and the passing of an Act of Parliament in 1877 authorising purchase by the Metropolitan Board of Works of the Common, as well as Bostall Heath *(see Abbey Wood 13)*, and Shoulder of Mutton Green, Welling. In 1900 it came under the control of the Metropolitan Borough of Woolwich, and in 1965 the London Borough of Greenwich.
>
> Winns Common, the part of Plumstead Common to the east of Lakedale Road, was named after Thomas Winn, who owned adjacent cottages and fields in the 19th century.

Though much is flat and grassed, there are some undulating areas and steep slopes, and a number of interesting natural features, including two ravines and a steep belt of woodland at the eastern end.

Perhaps the most memorable feature is *****The Slade (13A)**, a dramatic ravine with a picturesque lake at the bottom, part of a dried-up river bed. Best accessed at the head of Roydene Road, though there are several flights of steps leading down from the Common; also accessed by a slope leading down from the road called The Slade - from this point there are magnificent views across to the other side of the Thames.

There is another ravine, the **Bramblebury Ravine (13B)**, deep and very densely wooded, between Vicarage Park and Bramblebury Road. Best accessed by the flight of steps at the south end of Vicarage Park; the descent from the gate on Plumstead Common is very steep.

Behind the houses on the west side of Blendon Terrace is a strange outcrop of **puddingstone rock boulders (13C)**.

At the eastern end around **Bleak Hill**, steps of the Green Chain Walk lead steeply down a delightful forested slope from Grosmount Road to Wickham Lane. Further south Bleak Hill Lane leads to **Holly Cottage (13D)**, with a Gothic arch over the porch, probably mid 19th century. Here the Common falls away quite precipitously in a wooded cliff-face down to Kings Highway.

In the middle of Winns Common is a **prehistoric burial mound (13E)**, probably a Bronze Age barrow.

There are two **memorials** on the Common. One, in the west, between St Margarets Grove and Blendon Terrace, is a first world war memorial to the 8th London Howitzer Brigade of the Royal Field Artillery. The other, in the east, between Kings Highway and Swingate Lane, is a memorial to George Webb (headmaster of Burrage Grove Boys School) of 1896; now a squat granite pillar, it was originally taller and incorporated a fountain.

There are many good **views** towards the river, the best being from the headland **(13F)** on Winns Common between Riverdale Road and Purrett Road, embracing virtually the whole of Plumstead and Thamesmead.

**14. St Margarets School**, St Margarets Grove. A school of 1856, originally Plumstead Central School, still looking very much a village school. Note the strange tower with pyramidal roof and a metal fleche.

**15. Prince of Wales**, 111 Plumstead Common Road. An appealing late 19th century red brick pub with elegant Dutch gables and lively white stone dressings. The Dial Square Football Club, later to become the Arsenal Football Club, was founded here in 1886 *(see Introduction to Woolwich, page 12)*.

**16. Wrottesley Road.** This road, first laid out c1877, has some amazing late 19th century houses at its northern end. No 1 has eccentric decorative features, including multi-coloured tiling above the ground floor windows, and a tiled bargeboarded gable. No 7 and opposite nos 2, 4 and 14/16 have strong Gothic features.

**17. Vernham Road** has on both sides long and impressive red brick terraces with terracotta panels, of the 1890s. There are similar terraces of the same date in **Isla Road** and **Vambery Road**.

**18. 84/110 Plumstead Common Road**, a fine group of houses, in fact the oldest houses facing the Common. From west to east:

**Nos 84/100**, formerly called Ebenezer Terrace, an Italianate terrace of 1848.

**Unity Cottages**, nos 102/4, a basic brick pair of 1844.

**Nos 106/110**, a group of three villas of c1848 - no 106, brick; no 108, particularly attractive, stuccoed, with a strong Doric porch; and no 110, also stuccoed with a Doric porch, but with a later two storey bay to the left.

**19. Shrewsbury Villas**, 10/20 Plum Lane, an Italianate group of 1858. South of Vambery Road is a virtually similar group, **22/32 Plum Lane**, but built later, probably in the 1880s. Plum Lane was an old road leading down from Shooters Hill.

**20. 85/91 Genesta Road.** This reinforced concrete terrace in Le Corbusier style, by Berthold Lubetkin (of Bauhaus fame) and A.V. Pilichowski, was considered pioneering when built in 1935. It looks incongruous in this Edwardian and late Victorian neighbourhood, though it would have greater affinity in an area of Georgian terraces. Note the continuous projecting metal windows on the first floor, the small curved balconies on the second floor, and the ground floor 'pilotis' (or pillars).

**21. Plumcroft School**, Plum Lane. A London School Board school of 1903, comprising two buildings both with interesting features. The building to the north has an elegant slim belltower and on its south front facing Nithdale Road strange Flemish-style dormers. The building to the south also has a tall belltower, and its south front is quite eccentric, with a bold large central oriel. Both buildings have more solid and similar north fronts facing Genesta Road.

**22. Cherubim & Seraphim St Michaels Church**, Admaston Road. Very Gothic, originally the Mission Church of St Alban c1904.

**23. The Ship**, 205 Plumstead Common Road. An attractive white pub with a late 19th century appearance, but in fact totally rebuilt 1931.

**24. The Links**, Plumstead Common Road. A terrace of Co-op shops, with an amazing 'Rhine Castle' style clock tower of 1905, a prominent local landmark, above a half-timbered gable and a two-storey oriel.

**25. Plumstead Almshouses**, 53/57 Waverley Crescent. These surviving almshouses form a small eccentric group of 1896, with the upper floor extending as dormers into unusual Dutch gables. Similar groups at nos 49/51 and round the corner in Heavitree Road were destroyed during the war; they were rebuilt c1952 in a vaguely sympathetic style with strange though different gables.

**26. *The Old Mill**, Old Mill Road. A handsome stuccoed mid 19th century pub. It was originally an extension to a windmill, which was in use for grinding flour till 1853. The large stump of the mill, dating from 1764 and now converted to a house, still adjoins at the rear; there is an excellent view from the side of the pub.

**27. Plumstead Manor School**, Old Mill Road, formerly known as Kings Warren School. An attractive school of 1913 in classical style; note the dentilled cornice and dormers, and that alternate windows on the upper floor are pedimented. Behind to the north are a series of modern extensions, including a bridge over Heavitree Road, by the celebrated partnership of Powell & Moya 1973.

**28. Prince Albert**, 9 Old Mill Road. A handsome pub converted from three out of a terrace of four mid 19th century cottages. It originally occupied the central two cottages, but it absorbed the third in 1982. The Prince Albert, Plumstead Manor School and The Old Mill form an interesting group of buildings overlooking the Common.

**29. Church of St Mark**, Old Mill Road. This church of 1976 by David Bush replaced a building of 1902 destroyed during the war. The exterior is bleak and low-lying. The interior *(contact 0181-854 2973)* is pleasing, with much exposed brick. Note the small stained glass windows by John Hayward. The parish hall, probably c1910, survives alongside.

**30. Tormount Road.** This road, possibly unique in the London area, descends steeply through two hair-pin bends. Laid out c1896, lined by houses on both sides.

**31. Greenslade School**, formerly known as The Slade School. A powerful London School Board building of 1884 by Edward Robson. The elongated windows extending into the roof as tall dormers are a prominent architectural feature.

**32. Who'd a Thought it**, 7 Timbercroft Lane. An attractive pub, probably early 19th century, with a projecting ground floor c1878 and a modern extension to the right. The pub sign, a flying pig, is a recent idea.

**33. Wesley Hall Methodist Church**, Timbercroft Lane. A large red brick church of 1914, with great round-headed windows.

**34. Timbercroft School**, consisting of three separate classical buildings of 1906, with curved gables and dentilled cornices, and other decorative features. It is very similar in appearance to Deansfield School, Eltham.

**35. Church of the Ascension**, Timbercroft Lane. An Edwardian Gothic brick church of 1904, the present chancel added 1912; note the polychrome terracotta and intricate brickwork. The orientation of the church is to the south-west. Pleasant spacious **interior** *(contact the Vicarage, Thornhill Avenue, 0181-854 3394)* with nice brick patterns. A fine rood of 1920 under the chancel arch commemorates the first world war. The statue of Our Lady at the entrance to the Lady Chapel came from Holy Trinity Church, Beresford Square, Woolwich (built 1852, demolished c1960). The red brick vicarage opposite is of 1933.

**36. The Woodman**, 35 The Slade, a pleasing pub, mid 19th century with a later projecting ground floor.

**37. The Peoples Hall**, of the Evangelical Free Church, 38 The Slade, originally built 1880, its present appearance with great round-headed windows of 1902.

**38. Woolwich Cemetery.** The cemetery has two parts, separated by **Rockcliffe Gardens (38A)**, a rather neglected public park which was once quite picturesque. The older part has a main entrance in Kings Highway and another entrance in Camdale Road; it was laid out in 1856, and is spacious and beautifully landscaped. The later part, with its entrance in Camdale Road, was laid out in 1885; it commands views of the hilly areas around.

The older part is the more interesting. There is a rather sombre Gothic chapel with detached steeple, no longer in use. Note the large and impressive white Celtic cross commemorating the Princess Alice river disaster of 1878 off Tripcock Point (now part of Thamesmead) - "550 were drowned 120 were buried near this place". Note also the family grave of William Thomas Vincent 1920, who founded the Woolwich & District Antiquarian Society in 1895, on the main drive from Kings Highway up to the chapel; and the tombstone to Alexander McLeod 1902, a founder and first full-time secretary of the Royal Arsenal Co-operative Society *(see Woolwich 22)*, against the west wall.

**39. 1/4 Heath Villas**, two pairs with elliptical doorways, probably of the 1850s. Together with later buildings they form a distinctive edge to this part of the Common.

# PLUMSTEAD

## Gazetteer

### Section 'C' PLUMSTEAD HIGH STREET
*(See map on page 58)*

**40. \*\*St Nicholas Church.** The original parish church of Plumstead is partly early medieval. The best view is from the gateway to the south-west, where the oldest and most interesting parts, the south aisle (the original 12th century church) and the 17th century brick tower, are dominant. The south aisle is of ragstone and rubble, whereas the remainder of the church is of brick.

> The original church was built in the 12th century on a chalk spur jutting out into the marshland, and is now the south aisle; it is not known where the entrance was. In the 13th century transepts were added on both sides. In the 15th century a north aisle was added, destroying the north transept, and a doorway (now blocked) was built in the west wall. In the 17th century the tower was built into the west end of the north aisle.
>
> Following damage caused by an explosion at the Arsenal in 1907, the church was greatly enlarged by Greenaway & Newberry - the nave became the south aisle with a Lady Chapel added, the north aisle was rebuilt and enlarged to form the new nave, and a new chancel, north aisle and chapel, and south porch were added, all the work being completed by 1908. The south transept and the Lady Chapel were badly damaged by a bomb in 1945, and these parts of the church were not rebuilt during the restoration of 1959, when some important new furnishings were added.

On the exterior of the south aisle, two small round-headed windows and much of the south and west walls remain from the 12th century; there is a 14th century blocked doorway in the south wall, and a 15th century blocked doorway in the west wall. The large Gothic window in the west wall is of 1868, as are the two Gothic windows to the east of the porch (which is of 1908). The foundations of the south transept (probably c1230) can be seen on the outside; the outer wall and the window here are postwar. To the east of this are some rather elegant column shafts remaining from the Lady Chapel of 1908, which was destroyed during the last war and not rebuilt.

The battlemented tower of 1664 is of strong red brick and in a belated Gothic style, with strange brick tracery in the windows; it is similar to the tower of St Lukes Charlton. The remainder of the exterior belongs to the enlargement of 1908, and is rather dull; however, note the castellated turret at the north-east corner.

The \***interior** is of considerable interest *(contact 64 Purrett Road, 0181-854 0461, or 317 1025).* The south aisle, with the two Norman windows high up on the south wall, gives some impression of the 12th century church; note also the remains of a round-headed window arch in the south wall above the blocked 14th century doorway. In the east wall of the transept, the angle of a recess indicates the location of a 13th century squint. The arcade separating the south aisle from the nave is 15th century; the inner ring of the easternmost archway of the arcade formed part of the 15th century chancel arch and was rebuilt here 1908.

The rest of the interior, including the nave, chancel and north aisle, is all of 1908. The interior was restored after war damage by Thomas Ford in 1959, and from this date note: the altars and reredos (in the form of a triptych) by Stephen Dykes Bower, with its painting by Donald Towner siting the crucifixion on Winns Common, overlooking Plumstead and the River *(see 13F);* in the north aisle chapel, a nicely decorated baldacchino with a hanging pyx, a rare feature, also by Bower; a font by Bower in the south aisle; and the well-carved kneeling angels on the choir-stalls, now at the west end. The bright stained glass in the east window is a first world war memorial, by Martin Travers. There are a number of 17th, 18th & 19th century gravestones and wall tablets.

A few monuments and tombstones survive in the churchyard, of which the larger part is now a small park, St Nicholas Gardens.

**41. \*Plume of Feathers**, 282 Plumstead High Street. An early 18th century pub retaining much of its original structure and appearance. Early 19th century additions include the extension to the east with a fine oriel window, and the central entrance bay. At the rear the roof sweeps down steeply, and there is a late 19th century gabled dormer.

**42. The Prince of Orange**, 244 Plumstead High Street. An ornate pub of 1890, with an attractive ground floor.

Adjacent is **2 Rippolson Road**, a building of 1883, originally a stable for a farrier (or horseshoe-maker). Note the carved horseshoe above the entrance.

Opposite is **The Horse and Groom**, similar to The Prince of Orange but less ornate, also late 19th century.

**43. Plumstead Library**, an agreeable and harmonious red brick building of 1903, with gently bowed windows on either side of an almost monumental entrance. The library is on the ground floor; the upper floor is occupied by **\*Greenwich Borough Museum**, which was opened in 1919.

Introductory displays are on the landing and foyer of the Museum; they feature items from the collections which illustrate the wide-ranging interests of the founders, recent acquisitions, a 'Collectors Corner' for children, and an exhibition area. You then come to a magnificent painting, 'The Launch of the Royal Albert at Woolwich 1854', by George Chambers Jr. The gallery to the left has an area for temporary exhibitions and a permanent exhibition of pictorial displays and three-dimensional models of wildlife habitats in the area.

The gallery to the right has displays and exhibits relating to the history of the Borough; it is well set out chronologically going clockwise and has detailed explanations. The displays include prehistoric fossils and flint implements; pottery from the Roman cemetery found in the Dial Square area of the Royal Arsenal (note the face-jugs), and other Roman finds; substantial finds from the Romano-British settlement at Maryon Park, Charlton, and from the Roman building (almost certainly a temple) at Greenwich Park; some interesting Saxon bronze ornaments; glazed terracotta and clay floor tiles, a portion of a tomb-slab, and other remains from Lesnes Abbey; medieval pilgrims' badges; a wooden door from the original Philipot Almshouses, Eltham, 1694; a Georgian bow window from Powis Street; finds from excavations of the Palace of Placentia on the Royal Naval College site in Greenwich 1970-71; finds from recent excavations at the Royal Naval Dockyard; a magnificent mayoral chair made from the timbers of the Royal Albert 1855, presented to the Borough by the architect Thomas Dinwiddy 1901; household and kitchen furnishings from Victorian middle-class homes; etc. etc.

> The Museum is open Monday 1400 to 1900, Tuesday, Thursday, Friday & Saturday 1000 to 1300, 1400 to 1700. Closed Wednesday, Sunday and public holidays. Admission free. It is planned to relocate the Museum by 1998 to the Royal Arsenal site, where it will, jointly with Greenwich Local History Library, occupy Verbruggens House, the Dial Square Block, the Main Guard House, and (probably) the Royal Brass Foundry.

**44. The Volunteer**, 130 Plumstead High Street. A pub probably containing 18th century structure, its present appearance of 1861. The building was until 1859 the vicarage of the original parish church of St Nicholas. Attractive exterior and interior. Note the free-standing inn sign.

Adjacent are **136/142 Plumstead High Street**, an early 19th century group with modern shopfronts.

**45. Plumstead Fire Station**, a handsome classical building of 1913 with twin Ionic pilasters along the upper level facing the High Street.

**46. Council depot**, White Hart Road. The large site was opened in 1903 as a combined refuse destructor / incinerator and electricity generating station. Power generation ceased in 1923, incineration in 1965. The substantial complex of buildings, which is now used for storage and workshops, is of great interest.

At the entrance is a gatehouse and a weighbridge, both disused. Ahead are three adjoining buildings, the north hall, middle hall and south hall, all attractively styled in red brick with stone dressings; the south hall, to the right, smaller and later than the other two, has an old horse ramp leading to the upper floor. Go round the north of the complex and you come to the Office, an eccentric building with strange dormers and chimneystacks. Behind the Office is the **Tiled Hall**, with an imposing entrance at the eastern end; it is worth asking at the Site Management Office for permission to see the interior, which is covered in white tiles, is lit by a clerestory along the roof ridge, and has a full-width overhead travelling crane.

**47. Southern Outfall Sewer.** Constructed in 1862 as part of Sir Joseph Bazalgette's comprehensive London sewerage system, which was officially opened in 1865.

The sewer emerges from underground near Plumstead Station to run within an immense grassy embankment through Plumstead and Abbey Wood to the Crossness Sewage Works at Belvedere. A footpath, **Ridgway**, runs along the top of the embankment throughout the area and has recently been restored for public use. The section in Plumstead can be accessed from steps at the end of White Hart Road, and from Nathan Way in West Thamesmead Business Park.

**48. The Red Lion**, 95 Plumstead High Street. This pub probably contains early 18th century timber-framing. The exterior was rebuilt probably c1890, and tiling added to the ground floor. Attractive exterior (well restored in the 1980s) and interior.

**49. St Nicholas Centre**, Tewson Road. This building, probably of the 1880s, with its ornamented doorcase, was the former doctors quarters and is the sole building remaining of the Woolwich Union Workhouse infirmary, which opened in 1874 and became **St Nicholas Hospital** in 1929. The hospital closed in 1986 and was demolished in 1992; the rest of the site has been mainly developed for housing.

**50. Lakedale Centre**, of the Plumstead Christian Fellowship. It was built as Cage Lane Mission Church in 1879, and as the mission hall to the north has been demolished, it now occupies a key position at the junction of Lakedale Road and Brewery Road. The porch facing Brewery Road, with a great round-arched doorway topped by a circular window and pediment, is handsome; the side facing down Lakedale Road is considerably less so.

**51.** The site of the **North Kent Brewery** of Charles Beasley. It closed c1965 following acquisition by Courage. Some old walling along Brewery Road remains, probably of 1888, when the brewery was rebuilt.

**52. 18/22 Chestnut Rise.** A strange group of 1878, consisting of a central house with taller narrower houses on either side. Note the square bay windows, and Gothick red brick arches over the round-headed upper floor windows.

**53. Conway School.** A large and imposing London School Board school of 1897. Note particularly the south front (view from Gallossan Road) with its elegant twin cupolas. The north front on Bebbington Road is also impressive.

**54. St Patricks Church**, Hector Street. A red brick Gothic church of 1901, with a fleche. Until 1966 it was St Pauls Anglican Church, and was acquired by the Roman Catholic Church in 1969, actually the first such sale of a consecrated Anglican church and necessitating an Act of Parliament. The **interior** is spacious *(contact the presbytery at 1 Conway Road, 0181-854 0960)* with great Gothic arcades separating the nave from the aisles; the stained glass in the great east window is of 1923.

**55. St Patricks School.** The building on Conway Road was formerly St Patricks Church, a Roman Catholic church of 1893, in vivid red brick with a Romanesque facade; it has been St Patricks School Hall since 1969 *(see above)*. Behind on Griffin Road is the original school building of 1909, with nice red brick dressings. The presbytery at 1 Conway Road is of 1906.

**56. East Plumstead Baptist Church**, a large and powerful Gothic church of 1925, with a strange fleche. Spacious interior with an impressive wooden roof.

# PLUMSTEAD

## Suggested Walk

It is recommended that the suggested walk be followed in conjunction with the Gazetteer and the map, and that the Gazetteer be consulted at each location. Most locations described in the Gazetteer are covered; some locations have not been included, as they might add too much to the length of the walk.

The walk covers Sections 'A', 'B' and 'C'. The walk follows a more or less circular route, beginning and ending at Plumstead Station. Distance approx six kilometres; because of the length of the walk, consider breaking the walk into two parts, one commencing at Plumstead Station, the other perhaps at St Nicholas Church.

NB. Plumstead Museum is closed between 1 and 2 pm daily, Monday mornings, and all day Wednesdays, Sundays and public holidays. It is important to make an advance arrangement - see the Gazetteer - to view the interior of St Nicholas Church, and if possible it is worth including the interior of St Marks Church as well.

On leaving **Plumstead Station (1)**, note **Plumstead Radical Club (4)** opposite. Bear left to **The Lord Derby (5)**, then turn right up Griffin Road. Turn right along Glyndon Road and left in front of **The Prince Rupert (6)**, and bear right round to **St Johns Church (7)** on Earl Rise; note **South Rise School (8)** over to the left. Turn left up Robert Street to Brewery Road, noting the derelict **Brewery Road Chapel (9)** opposite, then bear right to **The Rose Inn (10)**; note the adjacent houses and the old waterworks wall.

Pass The Rose Inn, turn sharp left along Durham Rise, then sharp right up Manthorp Road. Turn right into Vicarage Park to see **The Old Vicarage (12)**, then continue up Vicarage Park to the edge of **Plumstead Common (13)**. Continue along St Margarets Grove, noting **St Margarets School (14)** on the right, till you reach the **Prince of Wales (15)**.

Cross the road and walk up **Wrottesley Road (16)**, turn left into **Genesta Road**, noting **nos 85/91 (20)** on the left. Look at the north front of **Plumcroft School (21)**, then walk round the corner into Nithdale Road to see the other side and the other building. Walk down **Plum Lane**, noting **nos 22/32** and **Shrewsbury Villas (19)** on the left. Turn left along **Plumstead Common Road** to see **nos 84/110 (18)**.

Cross the road onto the Common, and bear right round the back of the houses to see the **puddingstone rock boulders (13C)**. Continue to Blendon Terrace, turn right to Plumstead Common Road, then turn left. On reaching **The Ship (23)**, turn left and cross the road into Old Mill Road. Note **The Links (24)** across the Common. Continue to the pub **The Old Mill (26)**, and bear left for **Plumstead Almshouses (25)**. Return to Old Mill Road and turn left, passing **Plumstead Manor School (27)**, **Prince Albert (28)** and the **Church of St Mark (29)**; try to see the interior.

70

Continue to **Tormount Road (30)**, descend the hair-pin bends to Roydene Road, turn right to the Common and **The Slade (13A)**. Walk past the lake and continue up the slope of the ravine to **Greenslade School (31)**. (Alternatively, to avoid a steep descent and ascent, from the top of Tormount Road cross the Common, skirting the ravine, to the school.) Walk round the school and bear left to the pub **Who'd a Thought It (32)**, then return to the Common.

Turn right along the road The Slade, passing **The Woodman (36)** and **The Peoples Hall (37)**. Ahead is **Winns Common (13)**; follow the road called Winns Common Road between two sections of the Common. On the right is the **prehistoric burial mound (13E)**; to the left the houses facing the Common include **1/4 Heath Villas (39)**. Continue past Riverdale Road to the headland between it and Purrett Road for the view over Plumstead **(13F)**. Descend Purrett Road to Plumstead High Street, then turn right for the **Plume of Feathers (41)**.

Cross the road into St Nicholas Road to see **St Nicholas Church (40)**; try to see the interior. Retrace steps to Plumstead High Street, turn right and cross the road. Continue to the **Prince of Orange (42)**, the adjacent **2 Rippolson Road**, and the **Horse and Groom**.

Continue along Plumstead High Street to **Plumstead Library (43)**; visit **Greenwich Borough Museum** on the first floor. Continue, passing **nos 136/142** and **The Volunteer (44)**, until you reach **Plumstead Fire Station (45)** and the junction with Lakedale Road. (If you have time, go down White Hart Road opposite to the **Council Depot (46)** and **Southern Outfall Sewer (47)**, then retrace steps.) Continue along Plumstead High Street to **The Red Lion (48)**, then retrace steps to the junction.

Turn right up Lakedale Road to the **Lakedale Centre (50)**, bear right into Brewery Road and alongside the **North Kent Brewery (51)** wall, and turn right down Orissa Road to Conway Road.

Cross into Gallossan Road opposite, note **Conway School (53)** on the left, turn left into Bebbington Road, left into Mineral Street, and sharp left into Hector Street, passing **St Patricks Church (54)**. Turn left into Mineral Street, and right along Conway Road until you reach **St Patricks School (55)**. Turn right down Griffin Road, left along Plumstead High Street and you are quickly back at Plumstead Station.

# SHOOTERS HILL

## Introduction

The Romans built Watling Street, the road between London and Dover, across the top of Shooters Hill, and the main road today, the A207 to Dartford, still broadly follows its course. The slope is steep on the west side coming from Blackheath, but more gradual on the east side going towards Welling. The road was improved and widened by the New Cross Turnpike Trust between 1718 and 1817.

The summit of the hill at 132 metres (in Eaglesfield Park) is one of the highest points in Greater London, and its landmark, the water tower, is prominent from afar - on a clear day it can be seen from Tower Bridge, from Hampstead Heath, and from the North Downs. Nearer, from the centre of Blackheath, the hump of the hill looks impressive and dramatic.

## Early history

There was a beacon on the hill (its site now in the grounds of the Memorial Hospital) from at least the 16th century onwards. For many centuries the area with its extensive and dense woods was known as the haunt of highwaymen.

At the end of the 18th century there were two taverns, predecessors of the present Bull and Red Lion, a few houses and an extraordinary folly, Severndroog Castle. The largest house, Shrewsbury House, owned by the Earl of Shrewsbury, was on the north slope; its location was near the present Shrewsbury House, and Shrewsbury Park occupies part of the grounds. Only Severndroog Castle survives from this period.

From the early 19th century a hamlet had begun to grow; it later became a village, and can still readily be detected - around the church and its school, and on the opposite side of the road in Red Lion Lane (which was the original road to Woolwich), around the Red Lion, and in adjoining parts of the main road.

## Growth of housing

By the late 19th century a number of large houses had been built in the woods to the south - these included Castle House, Castlewood House, Jackwood House, Wood Lodge, Summer Court, Warren Wood (where the writer Enid Bagnold had lived 1903-20) and Falconwood House; all have now gone, and their grounds now form the major part of the Shooters Hill Woods. Of several smaller villas which were built nearby on the main road during the same period, only Holbrook House and Derby Villas survive.

On the northern slopes from the 1860s a number of houses, some with very ornate features, appeared in streets nearer Plumstead and Woolwich. Many of the houses of the Herbert Estate around Herbert Road were similar in style to Burrage Town further north.

Higher up the area to the north of the main road remained sparsely inhabited until this century. The housing nearer the summit was developed predominantly from the interwar period onwards.

## Shooters Hill Woods

The slopes to the south of Shooters Hill Road form an uninterrupted belt of woodland, comprising Eltham Common, Castle Wood, Jackwood and Oxleas Wood; and Shepherdleas Wood, in the Eltham area, is really a continuation of Oxleas Wood across Rochester Way. Much of these woodlands has been designated as a site of special scientific interest by the Nature Conservancy Council. They were purchased for the public by the London County Council between 1922 and 1938, and are now managed by the London Borough of Greenwich.

Large areas of the woods, particularly in Oxleas Wood, are classified as ancient woodland, ie. woodland where broad-leaved trees were not felled between c1600 and recent times. There is however an immense variety of planted trees, remaining from the grounds of demolished mansions. The dominant large tree is the oak (some over 200 years old), and there are examples of sweet chestnut, beech, hornbeam, birch, pine, wild cherry, alder and ash, as well as the rarer wild service tree. Sections of the woodlands are coppiced, ie. cut down regularly, no longer for timber (as was the case until the 1920s) but in order to encourage small trees and shrubs, and there are extensive clumps of hazel, hawthorn, rhododendron, dogwood, elder, willow, rose, fern, holly etc. There are numerous types of fungi; and the insect life includes species of beetles, bugs, spiders and flies which are rare in Britain.

## Fine views

As one would expect, there are fine views from many points in the area, and from several places one can on a clear day distinguish many landmarks of Central London.

The best views are from the top of Severndroog Castle, but it may not be easy to obtain access. Other good views are: towards Central London, from the top of Occupation Lane, from the small roundabouts in Moordown, and from the main road by the Samuel Phillips seat; to the north, from Shrewsbury Park; to the east, from Eaglesfield Park; and to the south, from the terrace in Castle Wood and from the former cafe in Oxleas Wood.

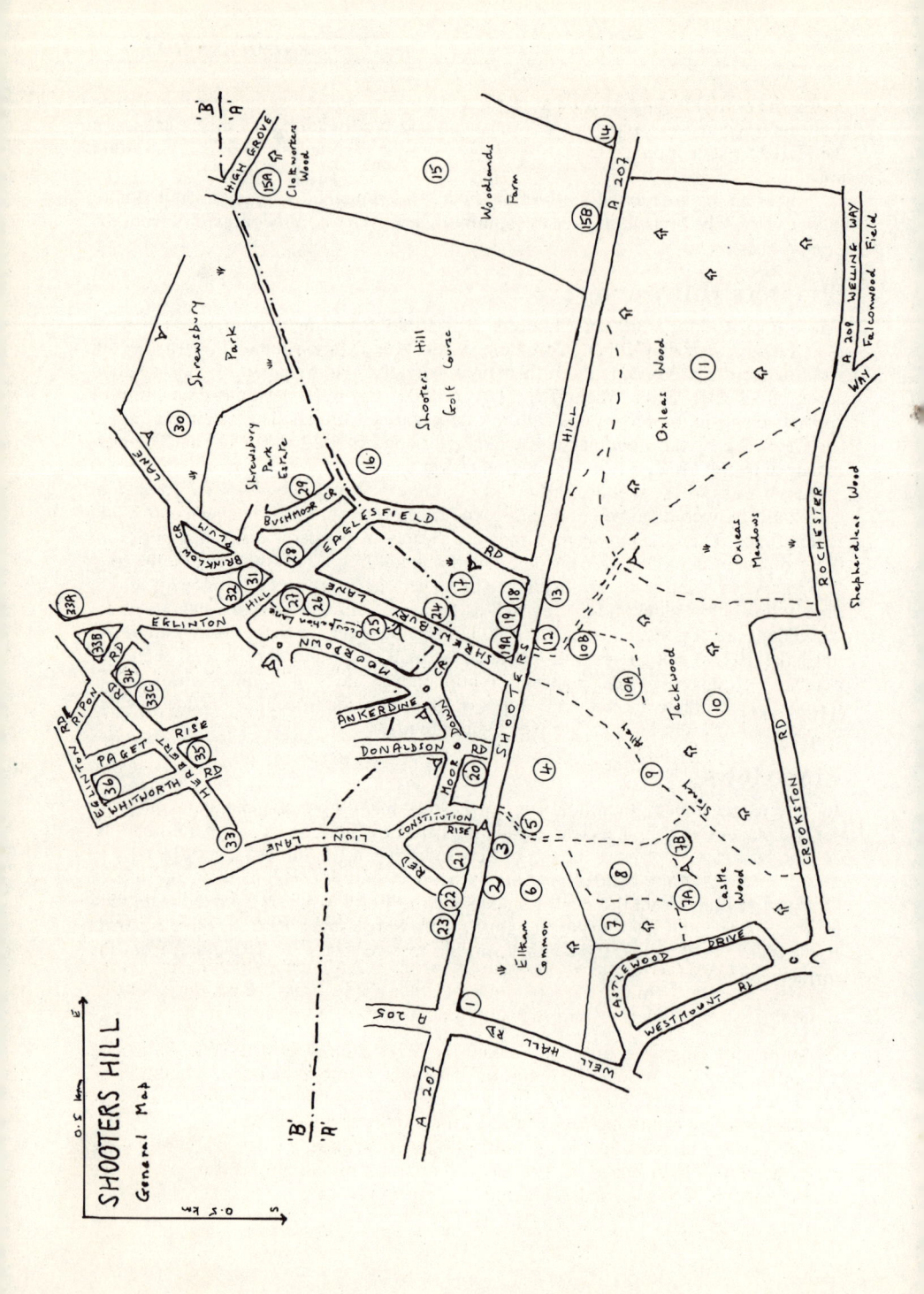

# SHOOTERS HILL
## General Map

# SHOOTERS HILL

## Gazetteer

### Section 'A' ROMAN ROAD & WOODLANDS

**1. Shooters Hill Police Station.** A red brick building of 1915 with prominent semi-circular bow windows overlooking the road junction. Alongside in Shooters Hill is the **Old Police Station,** a classical building of 1852 in yellow brick. They form an interesting pair.

**2. Christ Church.** A small Victorian Gothic church of 1856, the east end added in 1869. The exterior is unexceptional, but the **interior** *(contact 1 Craigholm, Shooters Hill, or ring 0181-856 5858)* is interesting, with the atmosphere of a village church. Note the fine east end stained glass window of 1869 and a series of unusual roofshields. In 1900 Temple Moore added a coloured chancel screen, two large figures of winged angels in the chancel, and the decorated cornices.

In the churchyard is a graceful Great War memorial cross of granite, and in front of this is the **Ypres milestone** - an 18th century milestone converted to a first world war memorial. It reads: '130 miles to Ypres, in defending the salient our casualties were 90,000 killed, 70,500 missing, and 410,000 wounded'. Note the modern **milestone** on the opposite side of the road, with replicas of 19th century iron plates reading '8 miles to London Bridge' and '7 miles to Dartford', which used to be on the Ypres milestone.

To the east is **Christ Church School**. The small central building is the old village school of 1857; the extensions on either side are postwar.

**3. The Samuel Phillips seat.** This memorial seat of 1893 has a nice lych-gate style roof. There was originally a drinking fountain, but only the pipe remains. Samuel Phillips (who lived at Castle House) was a founder of the firm Johnson & Phillips, manufacturers of submarine cables, which was in Victoria Way, Charlton. The inscription reads 'Write me as one who loves his fellow men' (which is also on his tomb in Charlton Cemetery, *see Woolwich Common 15*). From the main road at this point there is a fine **view** towards Central London.

**4. Memorial Hospital**, originally called the Woolwich & District War Memorial Hospital, later the Woolwich Memorial Hospital. A modest classical building of 1927, set in large grounds which include woodland similar to the adjoining Castle Wood. It was opened in memory of those killed in the first world war.

Just beyond the vestibule is the **Hall of Remembrance,** a small marble rotunda; note the enamelled roundel of The Good Samaritan by Gilbert Bayes, and stained glass windows of St Joan and St George.

## 76 - SHOOTERS HILL

**5. Castle House Lodge.** An early 19th century house, originally the lodge for Castle House (built 1823, demolished 1948), whose site is now in the grounds of the Woolwich Memorial Hospital.

**6. Eltham Common.** An area of open space, which links Woolwich Common (of which it used to form part) with the Shooters Hill Woods. It is partly grassed and partly wooded, this part sharing the characteristics of the adjoining Castle Wood. It was purchased from the Army by the London County Council in 1938.

**7. *Castle Wood.** *(See Introduction, page 73.)* An area of woodland, in part forming a dense pattern of tall trees. Its dominant features are Severndroog Castle *(see below)* and a large **rose garden (7A)**, which is on the site of Castlewood House (built 1870, demolished in the 1920s). The house and its grounds, including Severndroog Castle, were acquired by the London County Council in 1922.

Looking incongruous in the rose garden is a giant redwood tree. From the terrace above the garden there is a fine view southwards over Eltham towards the North Downs. To the east of the terrace is **Rose Cottage (7B)**, a highly ornamented house with rustic porch and great Dutch gables, probably of the 1870s, formerly the lodge for Castlewood House.

On the western edge of the Wood is a grassed area which covers a reservoir of 1920 *(see 17)*.

> Access to the Wood (and to Severndroog Castle) is by a driveway between the Samuel Phillips seat and Craigholm, which leads to a car park and footpaths onwards. There is another access footpath from Castlewood Drive to the south. There is a network of footpaths through the Wood.

**8. **Severndroog Castle.** A tall triangular battlemented tower with hexagonal angle turrets, an extraordinary Gothic folly surrounded by the trees of Castle Wood; it was built by Richard Jupp (architect of the main front of Guys Hospital) in 1784. The original main entrance is on the south-west face; other original entrance doors are blocked, with only the fanlights remaining; the smaller doors under the turrets were added later. Note the quatrefoil windows at the top of each turret, otherwise all windows are Gothic.

The inscription on the stone plaque over the original main entrance on the south-west face is transcribed on a tablet in a more legible position on the side facing north.

> Severndroog Castle was built by the widow of Commodore Sir William James to celebrate his naval exploits, in particular his capture in 1755 of the island fortress of Severndroog (no longer existing) off the Malabar Coast of India. At that time the Castle was just north of the grounds of the James mansion of Park Farm Place, Eltham (St Marys School, Glenure Road, now occupies the site). In 1870 the Castle became part of the grounds of Castlewood House, which was built on the wooded slopes below. The Castle and the House were sold to the London County Council in 1922.

From one of the turrets there are some of the finest **views** anywhere in London, unrestricted in all directions except to the north-east. The main room on the first floor has a fine ornamental plaster ceiling.

> It is not at present open to the public on any regular basis, but it is hoped that it may be re-opened in the near future. Phone the Greenwich Rangers Service on 0181-319 4253 for the latest information.

**9. Stoney Alley.** An old footpath running south from the main road, beginning just opposite the Bull pub and skirting the Memorial Hospital grounds. The southern part of the path forms the boundary between Castle Wood and Jackwood, and comes out in Crookston Road to the south. In the area near Rose Cottage are several very tall sweet chestnut trees.

**10. *Jackwood.** *(See Introduction, page 73.)* The north part of this large area of woodland, acquired by the London County Council in 1923, is dominated by the ornamental **terrace and gardens (10A)** of Jackwood House (built 1862, demolished in the 1920s) - note the fountain of 1873 with a lion's head. To the west of the terrace is an enclosed ornamental garden.

The site of the house is the area of flower-beds to the east of the terrace, and to the north of this site is a rather fanciful late 19th century house which was the staff quarters and stables. **The Lodge (10B)**, a house converted from two late 19th century cottages, one the lodge for Jackwood House, the other the gardener's cottage, is on Crown Woods Lane by the entrance into Jackwood.

> Access to Jackwood is by Kenilworth Gardens and Crown Woods Lane, which leads to a car park. Jackwood is then accessed by taking the footpath alongside The Lodge on Crown Woods Lane. There is a network of footpaths through the Wood. Visitors unfamiliar with the Wood are recommended to follow the signposts and markers for the Green Chain Walk.

**11. *Oxleas Wood.** *(See Introduction, page 73.)* A large wooded area, an outstanding example of surviving ancient woodland; it is amongst the oldest tracts of woodland in the London area. The woods are dense in places but interspersed with forest glades.

Oxleas Wood was acquired by the London County Council in 1934; beforehand much of the woods formed part of the grounds of Falconwood House (built 1867, demolished 1958), including the glades and, in the south-east corner of the woods, a stone-lined drinking pool for pheasants. (The driveway, now only a footpath, to Falconwood House still remains off the main road on the eastern slope, and the site of the House can be clearly identified at the end.)

> Access to Oxleas Wood is by Kenilworth Gardens and Crown Woods Lane, which leads to a car park. Beyond the carpark is Oxleas Meadows, and to the left Oxleas Wood. There are also footpaths into the Wood from further down the main road, and from Rochester Way and Welling Way to the south. There is a network of footpaths through the Wood. Visitors unfamiliar with the Wood are recommended to follow the signposts and markers for the Green Chain Walk.

From the former cafe near the entrance from Crown Woods Lane there are excellent views over **Oxleas Meadows** (which covers a large reservoir of 1983) eastwards over Sidcup with the North Downs in the distance. The former cafe is on the site of Wood Lodge (built c1780, demolished in the 1930s).

The woodland extends across Welling Way to the copse in **Falconwood Field,** and across Rochester Way to **Shepherdleas Wood.** These areas in Eltham were cut off from Oxleas Wood when the roads were constructed in the early 1930s.

**12. Holbrook House,** 162 Shooters Hill. A stuccoed villa c1838, which may incorporate some late 18th century structure; the bay window was added in 1862, and extensions to the rear in the late 19th century.

**13. Derby Villas**, 176 Shooters Hill, a multi-gabled, very Gothic building of 1861.

**14. We Anchor in Hope**, Bellegrove Road. An attractive brick pub of the 1850s, with a steeply pitched roof, looking more like a villa in its somewhat isolated location.

**15. Woodlands Farm**. A Co-op owned farm covering a large area to the east of Shooters Hill Golf Course. It is flanked by ancient hedgerows, which contain a wide variety of shrubs and plants. In the northern part of the farm is **Clothworkers Wood (15A)**, a small area of ancient woodland. There is a public footpath on the east side of the farmland, leading to the Dryden Road Open Space.

On the main road, surrounded by the farm, is **Woodlands (15B)**, a large and attractive house of 1886, with tiled upper floor and gables. To the west is a smaller house of the 1890s in a similar style, which was the **farmhouse** until the farm closed.

> Woodlands Farm was acquired by the Royal Arsenal Co-operative Society in 1920, and was until c1990 a working farm, one of very few surviving in Inner London. The RACS abattoir was located near Clothworkers Wood. There is a proposal to convert the whole area (including the two houses) into a 'social farm', with educational and ecological objectives, and with public access, which does not exist at present.

**16. Lowood**, Eaglesfield Road. A large house in stuccoed concrete of 1874; since 1925 it has been the clubhouse of the Shooters Hill Golf Club. The location of the house, with its wooded backcloth and the course sloping away, is magnificent. The east front, with its three distinctive gables, looks dramatic over the broad expanse of the golf course as one ascends the main road from the east.

**17. Eaglesfield Park.** This area of open space, on both sides of Eaglesfield Road, embraces the actual summit of the hill. There are sensational views towards the east over Erith, Bexleyheath and Bexley. Acquired by the London County Council 1908.

**18. *Water Tower.** A heavy fortress-like tower, octagonal and multi-coloured, of 1910, a prominent landmark which pinpoints Shooters Hill from afar. The detailing is extraordinary - note the triangular dormers, and on each face three round arches, below which are corbelling and elongated round-arched recesses with lancets. It was built to bring water to residents at the top of the hill; the water is forced up to the tower from a reservoir under Castle Wood *(see 7)* by a pumping station next to the Welcome Inn, Well Hall Road.

**19. A horse mounting block** with three steps, dating back at least to 1750. It is in front of the site of The Bull, a large and well-known tavern, built c1749 (possibly much earlier), and demolished in 1881. The block was re-erected here in 1929, but almost certainly the wrong way up.

Behind, and on part of the site of The Bull, is **157/9 Shooters Hill**, an amazing multi-gabled pair of 1907 with all sorts of ornamental flourishes, including blue brick diaper patterns and fantastic chimneys.

About 65 metres to the east is the present red brick pub **The Bull (19A),** of 1881, with good brick and terracotta work, and nicely curved bay windows. The date stone ('built 1749, rebuilt 1881') is over the original corner entrance, now bricked up. Note the sunflower motif on a bay to the left, and on the keystones above the upper floor windows. Just outside the door into the rear garden is another massive stone block, also probably c1750.

**20. The raised pavement** at this point on Shooters Hill, opposite the Memorial Hospital, indicates the original level and contour of the Dover Road before the gradients were eased by the New Cross Turnpike Trust c1817.

**21. The Red Lion.** A pub of 1902, replacing a much older building located slightly to the north. It is attractive externally and internally. Note the grotesque figure on top of the sharp corner gable. The pub is at the centre of **Red Lion Place,** an enclave of houses with a lot of character; the houses to the right are of 1886 and the houses to the left of 1902.

Adjacent but on the main road to the east are **53/57 Shooters Hill,** an interesting group. No 53 is a house c1835 with a modern shopfront, no 55 is of 1886, and no 57 (Prospect Cottage) is basically late 18th century, though its present facade with striking Gothick windows is probably c1816.

**22. Red Lion Lane.** This was the original road from Shooters Hill to Woolwich. The southern part is a tree-lined slightly winding village-type street, with considerable atmosphere. The west side consists mainly of long terraces of older houses. Note in particular: nos 124/144 c1902, with nice decorative features; no 126, of the 1840s, an attractive detached house with distinctive features; nos 98/102 (Elizabeth Cottages) and nos 50/68, both mid 19th century. The other terraces are late 19th century.

**23. Castlewood Centre,** originally Woolwich & Plumstead Cottage Hospital, and still in Health Service use. An unusual vernacular building of 1889, with a tile-hung upper floor and attractive decorative features. Note the foundation stone by the entrance.

In front, by the east driveway, is a **Board of Ordnance marker post** of 1808, the last such marker to survive in the area.

# SHOOTERS HILL

## Gazetteer

### Section 'B' THE NORTHERN SLOPES
*(See map on page 74)*

**24. 40 Shrewsbury Lane**, formerly known as Elmhurst Cottage. A weather-boarded cottage, rebuilt in 1975 as a replica of the original cottage of c1845.

**25. Occupation Lane.** This lane, almost rural in parts, winds round the back of Shrewsbury Lane to join Eglington Hill; it was laid out as a mews in the late 19th century, and has modern houses as well as old cottages. At the top it is flanked to the left by a stretch of 18th century walling (there is another stretch of 18th century walling between 59 & 61 Shrewsbury Lane), and there is a magnificent view westwards towards Central London.

**26. 91 Shrewsbury Lane**, a small stuccoed Regency-style house, probably of the 1870s, with an elegant iron balcony.

**27. 100 Eglinton Hill**, formerly known as Cheviot Lodge. A large and rather eccentric house c1868, with a large extension of 1882. It is difficult to discern the original house because of extensions and conservatories. Riverview Heights, a long block of flats, was built in the grounds in the 1950s.

**28. Shooters Hill Fire Station**, Eaglesfield Road. A handsome building of 1912 in Arts & Crafts style. Note the oriel windows, and the impressive skyline with closely packed dormers in the top storey (built as flats for firemen). The future use of the building is now in doubt.

**29. Shrewsbury House**, Bushmoor Crescent. A large building of 1923 in classical style; note the large front porch on Ionic columns, and to the rear a curved porch also with Ionic columns. It is located near the site of an older house with the same name (built 1789 for the Earl of Shrewsbury, leased in 1799 to the Crown for the young Princess Charlotte, daughter of the Prince Regent, demolished 1923). It is now in use as a community centre.

It is situated on the **Shrewsbury Park Estate**, an attractively laid out 'garden suburb' style estate with several greens, built in the grounds of Shrewsbury House in the 1930s.

**30. Shrewsbury Park.** An extensive park with a wooded area and wildlife sanctuary, its lower slopes giving excellent views over Plumstead, Thamesmead and the Thames. It was once part of the grounds of Shrewsbury House, which were purchased by the London County Council in 1928.

**31. A Bronze Age round barrow,** at the junction of Brinklow Crescent and Plum Lane. This prehistoric burial mound is the sole survivor of several on Shooters Hill, the others having been destroyed in building works in the 1930s.

**32. 133/155 Eglinton Hill** form an imposing group going downhill on the east side of the road. All houses have projecting bay windows through two storeys. Nos 133/143 are probably of the 1870s. Nos 145/7, of c1898, has attractive ornamental features, including a head within a medallion in the pedimented gable-end. Nos 149/51 are c1899, and nos 153/5 c1902.

**33. Herbert Road.** The Herbert Estate, which included the residential part of Herbert Road as well as streets on either side, was mostly developed from c1860 to c1880. Note:

    **The Lord Herbert Tavern (33A)**, no 47, an attractive classical pub c1870.

    **No 51 (33B)**, formerly called White Lodge, with corner turret and ornate doorway, of 1905.

    **Herbert Terrace (33C)**, nos 85/133, a pleasing group probably mainly of the 1870s, with a commanding location on an embankment above the road. The northern side opposite has many similar houses, which help to make the road form a pleasing ensemble.

**34. All Saints Church**, Ripon Road. A simple red brick church, rather Byzantine in style, with a thin but striking campanile. It was built by Thomas Ford 1957, replacing a church of 1881 destroyed during the war.

    The **interior** *(contact the Vicarage, 106 Herbert Road, 0181-854 2995)*, almost Greek Cross in plan, is strange and colourful, with green octagonal columns. There is a large mural of The Ascension by Hans Feibusch at the east end.

    The Vicarage opposite, 106 Herbert Road, is an attractive house c1875.

**35. St Josephs Church**, Herbert Road. A rather stark Victorian Gothic red brick Roman Catholic church, originally built as a Methodist Church in 1886. The church commemorated the establishment of a Methodist mission in China, and built into the exterior of the apse at the east end are a foundation stone and memorial stones to missionaries who died in China. The orientation of the church is now to the west.

    Pleasant raked interior *(contact the Presbytery next door, 135 Herbert Road, 0181-855 7657)*.

**36. Eglinton School**, Eglinton Road. A striking, multi-gabled school built by the London School Board 1885. A plaque on the front states 'On this site W E Gladstone delivered his last speech to his Greenwich constituents 1878' - it was in a public hall cum roller skating rink on the site.

# SHOOTERS HILL

## Suggested Walk

It is recommended that the suggested walk be followed in conjunction with the Gazetteer and the map, and that the Gazetteer be consulted at each location. Most locations described in both sections 'A' and 'B' of the Gazetteer are covered; some locations have not been included, as they might add too much to the length of the walk.

The walk begins and ends at the Police Station at the bottom of the west slope of Shooters Hill. It follows a more or less circular route, so can be joined at any point. Distance approx four kilometres. The walk will be appreciated best if taken on a clear day, because of the many fine views. There is quite a steep ascent up the main road at the beginning of the walk.

The walk can of course be extended by walks through the woodlands, though this may add considerably to the distance covered. Bear in mind that the footpaths can become very muddy at times.

NB. It is worth trying to make advance arrangements - see the Gazetteer - to view the interior of Christ Church.

From the **Police Station (1)**, proceed up Shooters Hill on the south side of the road, with **Eltham Common (6)** on the right. On reaching **Christ Church (2)**, try to see the interior, and note the war memorial and the **Ypres milestone** in front. Continue up the hill to the **Samuel Phillips seat (3)**; look back for the view towards Central London at this point, then take the access road immediately to the right. Pass **Castle House Lodge (5)** on the left, and enter **Castle Wood (7)**. Proceed ahead on the footpath to **Severndroog Castle (8)** and beyond, descending the steps to the **rose garden (7A)**. Return up the steps to the first terrace and turn right along the path to **Rose Cottage (7B)**.

Continue to the footpath ahead, which is **Stoney Alley (9)**. Follow the Green Chain Walk markers into **Jackwood (10)** until you come to the ornamental **terrace and gardens (10A)**. Continue past the gardens and take the footpath to the left until you come to **The Lodge (10B)**. Turn right into Crown Woods Lane and enter **Oxleas Wood (11)**. Continue to the former cafe for the view, then retrace steps along Crown Woods Lane, passing The Lodge, until you come out to the main road. Note **Holbrook House (12)** on the right.

Cross the road to the **mounting block (19)**, with **157/9 Shooters Hill** behind and **The Bull (19A)** to the left, then bear right past the **Water Tower (18)**, noting **Derby Villas (13)** opposite. Turn left into Eaglesfield Road, walk up into **Eaglesfield Park (17)** for the view to the east, then continue along Eaglesfield Road as it bears left to the crossroads, noting **Shooters Hill Fire Station (28)** on the right.

Bear right and cross to the **prehistoric burial mound (31)** on the corner of Plum Lane and Brinklow Crescent, then turn left to **Eglinton Hill**. Turn right downhill, noting **nos 133/155 (32)** on the right, then retrace steps to the top, noting **no 100 (27)** at the junction. Turn right along **Shrewsbury Lane**, passing **no 91 (26)**, until you reach the top of **Occupation Lane (25)** and its view. Continue along Shrewsbury Lane, noting **no 40 (24)** on the left, then turn right down Ankerdine Crescent to the roundabout, with its fine view, turn left along Moordown, and left again into Donaldson Road, then right onto Shooters Hill.

Walk along the **raised pavement (20)**, noting the **Memorial Hospital (4)** opposite, and descend the hill. Note on the right **53/57 Shooters Hill**, and **The Red Lion (21)** in the enclave of **Red Lion Place**, then turn right into **Red Lion Lane (22)**. Walk a short way down, at least to no 126, and retrace steps. Continue down the hill, passing the **Castlewood Centre (23)**, until you return to the Police Station.

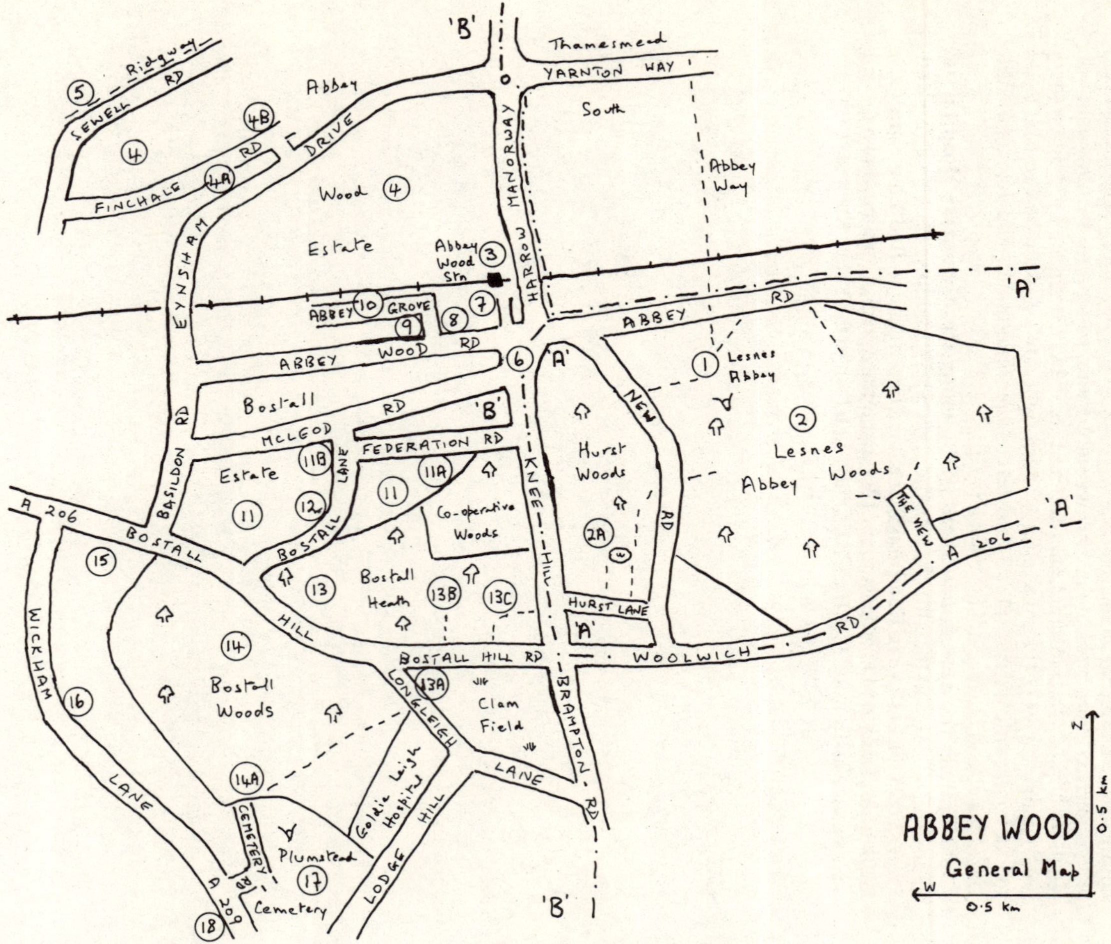


ABBEY WOOD

General Map

# ABBEY WOOD

## Introduction

The major part of Abbey Wood consists of a continuous belt of magnificent woodland, comprising Lesnes Abbey Woods in the east, and Bostall Heath and Bostall Woods in the west, separated by the old road of Knee Hill, which from 1888 until 1965 had been the boundary between London and Kent.

In a beautiful setting to the north of the Abbey Woods are the ancient ruins of Lesnes Abbey.

## Early history

The history of Abbey Wood begins with the foundation of the Augustinian Abbey of Lesnes in 1178. The buildings were largely destroyed soon after 1525 - it was dissolved by Cardinal Wolsey before the Reformation, because of its small size.

The abbey and the woodlands remained in private ownership until 1930, when they were acquired by the London County Council. The rest of the area remained largely farmland, very sparsely inhabited, until the beginning of this century. The arrival of the railway in Lower Abbey Wood, as early as 1849, had little impact.

## Bostall

Bostall was an old settlement whose site is now covered by the Bostall Estate. Bostall Heath and Woods were acquired for the public in the late 19th century.

The residential area called Bostall Heath, to the south of the Abbey Woods, is not included in the gazetteer.

## Growth of housing

The first houses were built in Lower Abbey Wood, to the south of the railway, in the 1880s. But the first large housing development in the area was the Bostall Estate, built by the Royal Arsenal Co-operative Society between 1900 and 1914, and considered a model estate at the time.

The London County Council built the Abbey Wood Estate to the north of the railway line in the 1950s, and in 1967 commenced building the large new town of Thamesmead, which adjoins and almost surrounds the Abbey Wood Estate to the north and east.

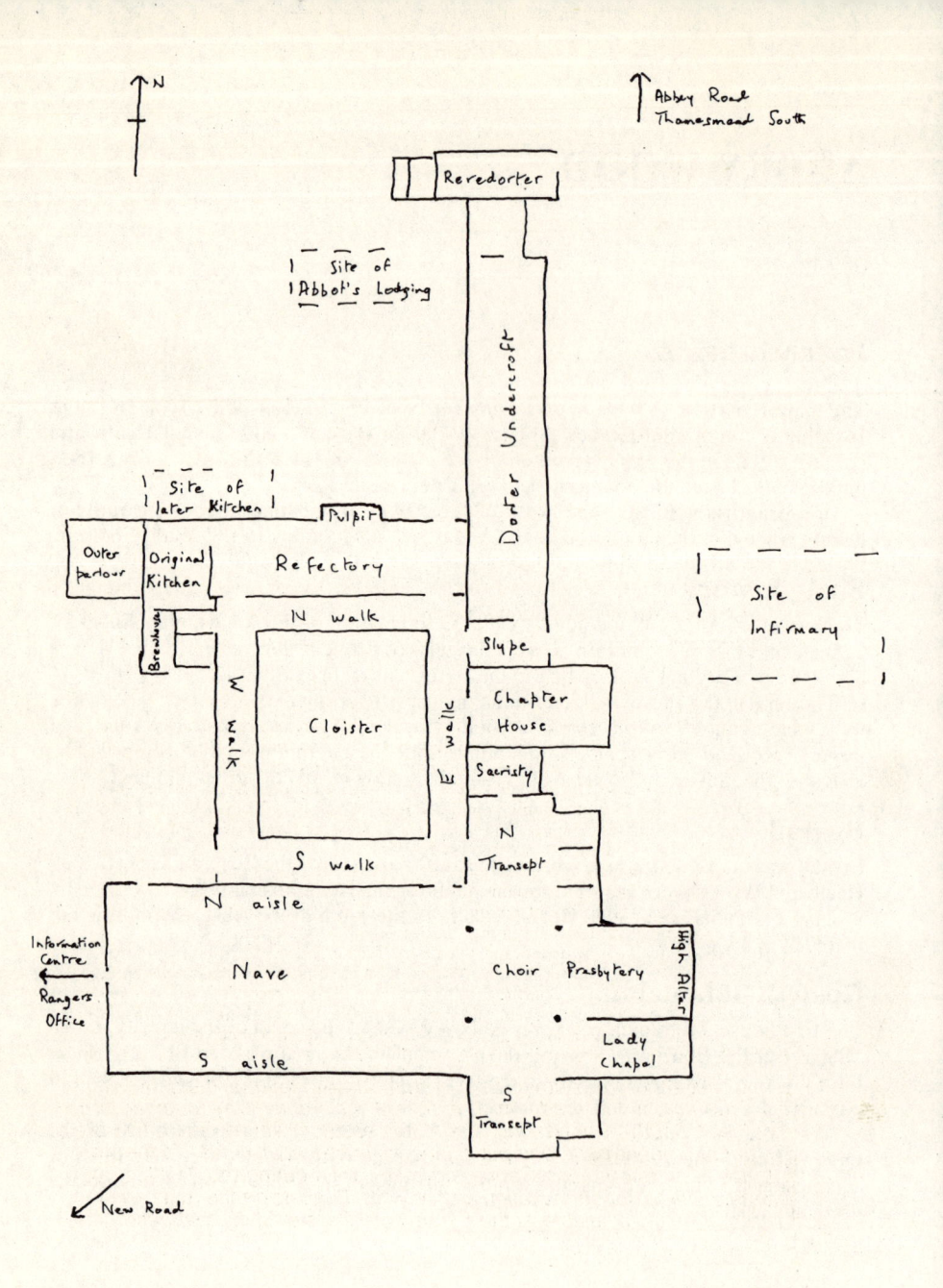

# Ground Plan of LESNES ABBEY RUINS

# ABBEY WOOD

## Gazetteer

### Section 'A' LESNES ABBEY & WOODS
(See map on page 84)

1. **Lesnes Abbey,** the ruins of a 12th century Augustinian abbey, beautifully situated on a sloping site with Lesnes Abbey Woods looming to the south. The ruins basically date from 1178 to 1200, though in the 14th century the Lady Chapel was added and the west wall of the cloister rebuilt. They are the only substantial medieval abbey remains in the southern London suburbs.

> The Abbey of St Mary & St Thomas the Martyr was founded in 1178 for the Augustinian or black canons by Richard de Lucy, Chief Justicier and royal deputy to Henry II, probably as an act of penance for his role in the murder of Thomas a Becket. He died the following year, and was buried in the Chapter House.
> 
> In its day the Abbey controlled the woods to the south, and the marshlands to the north up to the Thames; they maintained the river walls and drained the marshes. It was one of the first monasteries to be dissolved - by Cardinal Wolsey in 1525, before the Reformation, because of its small size; the buildings were then largely destroyed, leaving only the Abbot's house (which remained until 1845). In 1633 the site came into the ownership of Christs Hospital, and was used mainly for farming; it remained so until acquired by the London County Council in 1930.
> 
> The site was excavated by Sir Alfred Clapham 1909-13. (Finds from the excavations are in the Greenwich Borough Museum, Erith Museum, Bexley Museum, and St Johns Church Erith; a headless effigy of a knight of the de Lucy family and a famous early 13th century illuminated missal are in the Victoria & Albert Museum.)
> 
> In 1951 the ruins were restored and excavated further by F. C. Elliston-Erwood (commemorated by a plaque set into the footings of a nave pillar by the Woolwich & District Antiquarian Society), and the footings of the buildings reconstructed in many places, so one can readily comprehend the layout of the central monastic buildings and the abbey church. The infirmary, to the east of the ruins, and the Abbot's house, to the north of the ruins, have not been excavated.

*Access is best either from New Road, or from Abbey Road (ascend the stairs to the bridge across the road, which is part of the Abbey Way footpath from Thamesmead South). Car parking is normally easier in Abbey Road. The site is now part of a public park, and public access is free at all times. To the west of the ruins is an Information Centre, normally open during the daytime, and the Rangers Office (for consultation and advice). Leaflets on the ruins and the woods are normally available at the Information Centre. Many features of the ruins are labelled.*

*(See plan on page 86.)* From the Information Centre proceed directly to the west door of the Abbey Church and walk along the nave; note the bases of shafts along the north aisle, and at the end a grave slab. Walk up the steps into the choir (which was the tower crossing); note the substantial bases and shafts of the western piers. There are some original tiles where the south aisle leads into the south transept. From the choir continue straight ahead into the presbytery, and up the steps to the High Altar. Note on the right the Lady Chapel of 1371, which has an unusual tiled sunken chamber (used for storing holy relics etc).

Return to the crossing and walk down the steps, turn right and right again into the north transept. Note the three chapels, each with bases of shafts and a grave slab; beyond is the sacristy. From the north transept walk down the steps into the east walk of the cloister; note on the left some original tiles leading to the north aisle. Turn right, passing the book locker and a long stone bench which retains some original tiles, to the entrance to the Chapter House, which has reconstructed wall seating.

Continue along the east walk of the cloister and you immediately come to the slype (or passage), leading to the infirmary doorway. Beyond was the Infirmary, which has not been excavated; however, the footings to the left may have been connected with the Infirmary. Return to the cloister, and to the right are stairs leading up to the dorter (or dormitory). Walk down the steps to the undercroft of the dorter; note the two round headed windows in the taller west wall. Beyond the room at the end of the dorter is the reredorter (or latrines), with two deep pits.

Return to the cloister outside the dorter, entering through a modern Gothic doorway. Turn right along the north walk, which is alongside the ruins of the refectory. The high north wall of the refectory has clear remains of a staircase, lit by two tiny lancet windows, which led to the refectory pulpit. At the end of the refectory note the mulberry tree outside, which was near the site of the Abbot's House (which has not been excavated); and in the north-west corner, a serving hatch from the kitchen, which was outside the cloister. The original kitchen, however, was the room to the west of the refectory; beyond it was the outer parlour, and to its south an outer room was the brewhouse.

Turn along the west walk of the cloister; at the end turn right through the 14th century doorway, which is well-preserved. Note along the north wall of the nave some holes which were used for wooden supports for the pentise, or covered walkway, which led to the western processional door. Go through this doorway and back to the west door of the church.

On a terrace beyond the flower beds to the south is the well (now covered), from which water was conveyed to the site by leaden pipes; the well was fed by a pool in the south of the woods which has now dried up.

Depressions on either side of the site were used by the Abbey as a fish-pond (to the west) and a dew-pond (to the east).

A good view of the ruins can be obtained by ascending the steps into the woods behind the High Altar.

2. **\*\*Lesnes Abbey Woods.** An extensive area of rolling woodland, interrupted by deep valleys, some with extremely steep slopes. The overall effect is extremely picturesque. The woods were acquired by the London County Council at the same time as the abbey ruins in 1930, and are largely classified as ancient woodland. The woods also incorporate **Hurst Woods**, between New Road and Knee Hill.

There is a wide variety of trees, the dominant large trees being the sweet chestnut and the oak. There are also large groups of birch, ash, hornbeam, wild cherry, hawthorn, maple, hazel, and several wild service trees.

*Although the woods are dense and precipitous in places, there is a good network of well-surfaced paths. A self-guided trail to the woodlands of just over three kilometres may be obtained at the Information Centre near the Abbey ruins, and first time visitors are strongly recommended to follow this trail. Bear in mind that it includes some quite steep ascents and descents.*

The main places of interest, all included in the trail, are as follows:

(i) Three large fenced enclosures, immediately south of the abbey ruins, which protect the famous spring displays of wild daffodils, bluebells and wood anemones. In the middle enclosure is a separate fenced area containing some rich **fossil beds**; the fossils most commonly found are shells and sharks teeth, which may date back 56 million years, when the climate was tropical and the London area was covered by a warm shallow lagoon. *Authorisation to enter may be obtained at the rangers office.*

(ii) A **chalk pit**, deep and dramatic, where chalk was excavated before 1930 for use on the farmland around the Abbey site.

(iii) In Hurst Woods, a beautiful ornamental pool, called **Pine Pond (2A)**. It was created in the late 19th century as part of the grounds of Hurst House, which was located to the south of Hurst Lane. The pond can also be readily accessed by footpaths leading from Hurst Lane.

It is also worth entering the woods from the south, at the end of The View, off Woolwich Road. The main path on the right leads after a short distance to an attractive area of heathland. The path on the left leads quickly to a ridge, with steep and delightful ravines on both sides; 'giant steps' lead down to the further ravine.

# ABBEY WOOD

## Gazetteer

### Section 'B' LOWER ABBEY WOOD & BOSTALL
*(See map on page 84)*

**3. Abbey Wood Station.** A modern station with a striking design, its roof swooping up to an acutely angled point at the entrance. It was built in 1987 to replace an earlier building. The station was originally opened in 1849.

**4. Abbey Wood Estate.** A large estate, built by the London County Council between 1956 and 1959. There is a strong feeling of isolation - it is cut off to the north by the Southern Outfall Sewer, to the west by allotments, and to the south by the railway; to the east it is separated from Thamesmead South by Harrow Manorway. The only road access is by flyovers over the railway - Eynsham Drive in the west and Harrow Manorway in the east.

In Eynsham Drive is the centre, with a small shopping parade, library and **William Temple Church (4A)**, a modern church of 1966 with a thin spire and bright stained glass in the interior *(contact 5 Finchale Road, 0181-310 5614)*.

To the north, in Finchale Road, is **St Davids Church (4B)**, a Roman Catholic church of 1964 with a colourful figure of St David on the entrance wall; the interior *(contact 138 Godstow Road, 0181-311 2727)* has bright stained glass.

**5. Southern Outfall Sewer.** Constructed in 1862 as part of Sir Joseph Bazalgette's comprehensive London sewerage system, which was offically opened in 1865.

The sewer runs within an immense grassy embankment through Plumstead and Abbey Wood to the Crossness Works at Belvedere. A footpath, **Ridgway**, runs along the top of the embankment throughout the area and has recently been restored for public use. The section in Abbey Wood can be accessed from steps at the west end of Sewell Road, and also in the east near the footbridge over the Thamesmead Spine Road.

**6. The Harrow Inn.** An impressive pub with deep eaves, of 1860.

**7. The Abbey Arms**, Wilton Road. A pub, basically c1860, but considerably altered when rebuilt after a fire in 1900.

**8. Palanga House**, 133 Abbey Wood Road. A distinctive house of 1882, the oldest domestic building in Lower Abbey Wood. The adjacent **Rose Lea Villas**, 129/131 Abbey Wood Road, of c1885, also has distinctive features, and together they form an interesting group.

**9. Church of St Michael & All Angels**, Abbey Wood Road. A bulky but rather grand red brick church, by the firm of Sir Arthur Blomfield & Son 1908. The interior *(contact theVicarage, Conference Road, 0181-311 0377)* is spacious and very Gothic.

**10. Church of St Benet**, Abbey Grove. An impressive Roman Catholic church of 1909, with a great romanesque-arched doorway and a triplet of windows above separated by bulbous Saxon style pillars. Unremarkable interior, altered in the 1960s. The presbytery *(contact 0181-211 2594)* next door at no 31 is in similar style and forms an integral part of the building.

**11. Bostall Estate.** This estate under the shadow of Bostall Heath was built by the Royal Arsenal Co-operative Society *(see Woolwich 22)* between 1900 and 1914. It is bounded by Bostall Heath, Basildon Road, Abbey Wood Road and Knee Hill, with the main road McLeod Road running through. The estate consists of long terraces in varied styles, and many houses have ornamental flourishes and distinctive brick patterns. There has been considerable extension and infill since the last war, particularly in the western part, but the area retains a distinct Edwardian atmosphere. The estate is now mostly owned by a housing association.

An old chalk mine in Federation Road was used during the construction of the estate. The **Federation Day Centre (11A)**, formerly the Federation Hall, was the works dining hall. In the south-west corner of the grounds is the sealed top of the chalk mine, with a grill to allow passage to a colony of bats. The mine is 20 metres below ground; it was finally sealed c1960. *Ask permission from the Manager before looking around, or ring 0181-311 8519 in advance.*

The Co-op supermarket in McLeod Road has on the side facing Bostall Lane a splendid ornamental **plaque (11B)** of 1900 commemorating the commencement of the building of the Estate. There is also a smaller tablet commemorating the opening of the first Co-op shop there in 1912.

> Two large farms to the north of Bostall Heath, Bostall Farm and the adjoining Suffolk Place, were acquired by the Royal Arsenal Co-operative Society in 1886 and in 1899 respectively. In 1900 it was decided to convert the land to a housing estate. Building started in 1900, and continued to 1909; it resumed in 1912 but stopped in 1914 after 1052 houses had been built. The Caravan Club site, in the beautiful parkland setting of Co-operative Woods on Federation Road, was the works site during construction of the estate. Many road names in the area have Co-op associations.

**12. Alexander McLeod School**, originally known as Bostall Lane School, situated on the corner of Bostall Lane and Fuchsia Street. An impressive though rather heavy London School Board building of 1903, relieved by the balustrades and urns on top of the central section (best seen from the rear). Alexander McLeod was a founder and the first full-time secretary of the RACS *(see also Woolwich 22)*.

**13. *Bostall Heath** consists of heathland with gorse and broom at the top of Bostall Hill, and dense woods and deep ravines on the steep slopes to the north. The heath stretches across Bostall Hill to include **Clam Field**, a grassed open space fringed by belts of trees.

> Bostall Heath was acquired for the public by the Metropolitan Board of Works in 1877. As in the case of Plumstead Common and Shoulder of Mutton Green, Welling, which were acquired at the same time, this followed attempts by Queens College Oxford, which owned all these lands, to deny public access *(see also Plumstead 13)*. Clam Field was acquired by the London County Council in 1894.

The old **Heathkeeper's Lodge (13A)** at the corner of Bostall Hill and Longleigh Lane, a rather fanciful building with tiled upper floor, was built 1880 by the Metropolitan Board of Works. Opposite is a horse trough, late 19th century.

In the south-east three buildings occupy enclaves on the Heath: **Greenwich & Bexley Cottage Hospice (13B)**, a handsome building of 1994 with great sloping roofs and tiled gables, on the site of Shornells, a house of 1873 which became a training centre and guest-house for the RACS *(see Woolwich 22)* and was destroyed by fire 1989; **Bostall House**, modern, on the site of a mid 19th century house; and **The Belvedere Private Clinic (13C)**, formerly called **The Cottage**, where the brewer Charles Beasley *(see Plumstead 51)* lived from c1882 to c1923, a large and rather eccentric mid 19th century building, much altered, with fine bay windows, bargeboarding and other decorative features.

**14. *Bostall Woods.** A picturesque area of woodland, dense in places but interspersed with forest glades, on the slopes of Bostall Hill. There is a wide variety of trees, the dominant large trees being the oak, sweet chestnut and birch.

> The woods were formerly known as Old Park Wood, and included the grounds of Old Park House and Goldie Leigh Lodge, both early 19th century mansions. The woods were purchased by the London County Council in 1892 and were renamed Bostall Woods, and the houses were eventually demolished.
>
> Part of the woods was used from 1902 as Goldie Leigh Cottage Homes for children, a large complex which later became the Goldie Leigh Hospital. This closed in 1988, and the future of the site is now uncertain.

The site of Old Park House is now a glade located between the Green Chain Walk and the path along the boundary of Goldie Leigh Hospital; it is best approached by following the Walk signpost from Longleigh Lane.

**Woodside Cottage (14A)**, the house c1902 at the end of Cemetery Road, was a lodge alongside a driveway to Goldie Leigh Hospital; the old driveway, flanked by tall lime trees, can be reached by taking the footpath beyond the lodge and parallel to its garden for about 100 metres, then descending some steps to the right.

Under the eastern edge of the woods is a network of chalk mines, which were in use until the mid 19th century.

**15. Maybloom Club**, Bostall Hill. A grand classical building, built as Plumstead Workingmens Club c1912, which became the Maybloom Club, another workingmens club, in 1926. It has a fine frontispiece with balustrade and pediment, and rows of round-headed windows on either side.

**16. St Pauls School**, Wickham Lane, formerly Oakmere School. A large and splendid building, with tower, cupola and many ornate features, front and rear. It was built by the London School Board c1903, primarily for children at the Goldie Leigh Cottage Homes *(see 14)*. Modern extension to the north.

**17. Plumstead Cemetery**, Cemetery Road. This cemetery of 1890 occupies a spectacular hillside site, with magnificent views, particularly of the adjoining Bostall Woods. The arched gateway is echoed by the porte-cochere between the chapels. The larger chapel c1898 is in an ornate Gothic style with a tall spire. Nearby is a pink obelisk to men who were killed in explosions at the Royal Arsenal in 1903.

**18. The Foresters Arms**, Wickham Lane. A pleasing pub, basically c1860, but considerably altered at the front in 1874 and at the side in 1890.

# Bibliography

including books and publications consulted, and books recommended for further reading, especially for information on local history and architectural detail

*London 2: South*, by Bridget Cherry & Nikolaus Pevsner (Buildings of England series, Penguin Books, 1983)
*Handbook to the Environs of London*, by James Thorne (1876, republished 1970)
*The Industrial Archaeology of South East London* (Goldsmiths College Industrial Archaeology Group, 1982)
*Charing Cross to Dartford*, by Vic Mitchell & Keith Smith (London Suburban Railways, Middleton Press 1990)
*The North Kent Line*, by R. W. Kidmer (Oakwood Press 1977)
*Green Chain Walk*, leaflets nos 1 & 2
*The Records of the Woolwich District*, by W. T. Vincent (1890)
*Warlike Woolwich*, by W. T. Vincent
*The Woolwich Story 1890-1965*, by E. F. E. Jefferson
*The Royal Arsenal Woolwich*, by Wesley Harry (Ministry of Defence, 1987)
*Royal Arsenal Woolwich*. by the Royal Commission on Historical Monuments (1994)
*Royal Arsenal Woolwich an Archaeological Study* by Mills Whipp Partnership (1995)
*The Woolwich Mess*, by Col Alfred Burne (R.A. Institution, 1971)
*Woolwich Reviewed*, by Julian Watson (Greenwich Libraries, 1986)
*Old Ordnance Survey Maps*, published by Alan Godfrey - Woolwich 1866, 1914; North Woolwich 1869, 1894; Plumstead 1914; Plumstead Marshes 1894; Shooters Hill 1866, 1914; Charlton 1867, 1914
*Woolwich Architectural Heritage Trails* (Greenwich Tourism & Greenwich Mural Workshop 1994)
*Churches in the Hundred of Blackheath*, by L. A. J. Baker (Greenwich & Lewisham Antiquarian Society, 1961)
*Free For All*, a celebration of 100 years of the Woolwich Free Ferry, by Julian Watson & Wendy Gregory (Greenwich Libraries, 1989)
*Guide to the Museum of Artillery at the Rotunda* (1976)
*The Co-operative Way*, by Alfred Dennett (Royal Arsenal Co-operative Society)
*Looking Back at Woolwich*, by Ron Roffey (CWS South-East 1994)
*St Nicholas Plumstead* - a history of Church & Parish, by Stanley Henwood (1972)
*Shooters Hill*, by A. H. Bagnold (Christ Church Gazette, 1938)
*Aspects of Shooters Hill* (Shooters Hill Local History Group, No 1 1984, No 2 1989)
*Nature Conservation in Greenwich* (London Ecology Unit, 1989)
*Nature Trails to Oxleas Wood; Jackwood / Castle Wood* (Gordon Teachers Centre)
*Severndroog Castle & Sir William James* (Eltham Society, 1984)
Various articles and notices in Proceedings of the *Woolwich & District Antiquarian Society*, and in Newsletters of the *Greater London Industrial Archaeology Society*

All the above publications, and of course many more books, maps and documents, can be consulted at the **Greenwich Local History Library**, Woodlands, Mycenae Road, London SE3 (phone 0181-858 4631).

# INDEX

(Gazetteer references - W = Woolwich, RA = Royal Arsenal, WC = Woolwich Common, P = Plumstead, S = Shooters Hill, A = Abbey Wood

## Architects, Artists, Engineers
Charles Bailey - RA 13
Thomas Bailey - W 78
Gilbert Bayes - S 4
Sir Joseph Bazalgette - P 47; A 5
John Bell - WC 2
Stephen Dykes Bower - P 40
Sir John Burnet, Tait & Partners - W 16
David Bush - P 29
William Butterfield - W 49
George Chambers Jr - P 43
Henry Hudson Church - W 15, 17, 17A
Sir Ninian Comper - W 49
Alfred Drury - W 22
Hans Feibusch - S 34
Sir Maurice Fitzmaurice - W 31
Thomas Ford - P 40; S 34
Julia St Clair Forde - W 81
Sir Douglas Galton - WC 10
Count Victor Gleichen - WC 17
Greenaway & Newberry - P 40
Greenwich Mural Workshop - W 3B, 20, 25
Joseph Gwilt - W 52
Nicholas Hawksmoor - RA 4, 6
John Hayward - P 29
Richard Jupp - S 8
Theodore Komisarjevsky - W 23
Berthold Lubetkin - P 20
Thomas Milnes - RA 12
Temple Moore - S 2
David Murray - RA 13, 16
John Nash - WC 19
Vong Phaophanit - W 58
A. V. Pilichowski - P 20
Frederick Pomeroy - W 11
Powell & Moya - WC 14; P 27
Augustus Pugin - W 9
Edward Pugin - W 9
Rendel, Palmer & Tritton - W 58
John Rennie - W 42G
Edward Robson - W 43; P 31
Sir Giles Gilbert Scott - WC 2, 16
John Oldrid Scott - W 41
Sir Alfred Brumwell Thomas - W 11
Donald Towner - P 40
Martin Travers - P 40
Sir John Vanbrugh - RA 3, 4, 6
William Wailes - W 9
George Frederick Watts - WC 2
Geoffrey Webb - W 11
Christopher Whall - WC 9A

Martin Williams - W 1
James Wyatt - RA 8, 14; WC 2, 9
Lewis Wyatt - RA 8, 14
Thomas Wyatt - WC 3

## Churches, places of worship
Academy Chapel - WC 9A
All Saints - S 34
Ascension - P 35
Former Baptist chapels - W 7; P 11
Cemetery chapels - WC 15; P 38; A 17
Cherubim & Seraphim St Michaels - P 22
Christ Church - S 2
East Plumstead Baptist - P 56
Garrison churches - WC 3, 9A
Gurdwaras - W 5, 14
Lakedale Centre - P 50
Lesnes Abbey - A 1
Peculiar Peoples Chapels - P 9, 11
Peoples Hall - P 37
St Benet - A 10
St Davids - A 4B
Former St James Church - W 83
St Johns - P 7
St Josephs - S 35
St Mark - P 29
St Mary Magdalene - W 41
St Michael & All Angels - W 49; A 9
St Nicholas - P 40
St Patricks - P 54
St Peter the Apostle - W 9
St Thomas - W 52
Trinity Methodist - W 81
Wesley Hall Methodist - P 33
William Temple Church - A 4A
Woolwich Congregational - W 38
Woolwich & District Synagogue - W 6
Woolwich Mosque - P 2

## Housing developments
Abbey Wood Estate - A 4
Barge House Road - W 32F
Bostall Estate - A 11
Connaught Mews - WC 1
Greenhill Courts - WC 23
Herbert Estate - S 33
Plumstead Almshouses - P 25
Red & Cambridge Barracks - W 47
Royal Herbert Pavilions - WC 10
Shrewsbury Park Estate - S 29
Woolwich Common Estate - WC 8
Woolwich Dockyard Estate - W 42B/D

# INDEX - 95

## Industrial archaeology
Callis Yard - W 21
Cannon etc - W 47A; WC 2, 9, 18, 19, 20, 22
Chalk mines - A 2, 11A, 14
Co-op Movement - W 22, 42; P 1, 24; A 9, 11
Council depots - W 21; P 46
Horse mounting block - S 19
Horse troughs - W 26; WC 7; A 13A
Kent Waterworks - WC 11; P 10
Letter boxes - W 32H; WC 9, 11
London Teleport - W 32A
North Kent Brewery - P 51
Rail sidings - W 42; RA 4, 8, 15, 16, 19; P 1
Railway Stations - W 1, 32, 36; P 1; A 3
Railway tunnels etc - W 1, 36, 54, 56
Raised pavement - S 20
Riverside walks - W 32B, 35, 42D
Royal Arsenal - W 26, RA 1-22
Royal Artillery - WC 2, 4, 6, 9, 16A, 20, 21
Royal Naval Dockyard - W 42
Russian submarine - W 59
Sandpits - W 1, 36, 54, 55
Southern Outfall Sewer - P 47; A 5
Telephone kiosks - WC 2, 16
Thames Barrier - W 58
Water Towers - WC 11; S 18
Westminster Industrial Estate - W 62
Windmill - P 26
Woolwich Building Society - W 2
Woolwich Foot Tunnel - W 31
Woolwich Free Ferry - W 30
Woolwich Power Station site - W 35A

## Leisure
Coronet Cinema - W 40
Eauzone / Tram Shed - W 3B
Greenwich Young Peoples Theatre - W 83
Old Granada - W 23
Waterfront Leisure Centre - W 33
Workingmens Clubs - W 5; P 4; A 15

## Museums
Great Eastern Railway Museum - W 32H
Greenwich Borough Museum - P 43
Museums of Artillery - WC 9, 19

## Parks, woods, open spaces
Bostall Heath - A 13
Bostall Woods - A 14
Castle Wood - S 7, 8
Charlton Cemetery - WC 15
Charlton Sandpit - W 55
Clam Field - A 13
Eaglesfield Park - S 17
Eltham Common - S 6
Hurst Woods - A 2
Jackwood - S 10
Lesnes Abbey Woods - A 2
Maryon Park - W 54

Maryon Wilson Park - W 51
Oxleas Wood - S 11
Plumstead Cemetery - A 17
Plumstead Common - P 13
Rockcliffe Gardens - P 38A
Royal Victoria Gardens - W 32D
St Marys Churchyard - W 41
Shrewsbury Park - S 30
Winns Common - P 13
Woodlands Farm - S 15
Woolwich Cemetery - P 38
Woolwich Common - WC 12

## People
Charles Beasley - P 51; A 13C
Col Albert Borgard - WC 2
Richard Bowater - W 36; WC 2
Sir Alfred Clapham - A 1
Tom Cribb - W 41
General Sir Alexander Dickson - WC 2
F. C. Elliston-Erwood - W 55; A 1
Sir William James - S 8
Richard de Lucy - A 1
Alexander Mcleod - W 22; P 38; A 12
Henry Maudslay - W 41
John de Morgan - P 13
Pattison family - W 1, 83
Sir Flinders Petrie - W 55
Samuel Phillips - WC 15; S 3
Jan & Pieter Verbruggen - RA 2
W. T. Vincent - P 38
George Webb - P 13
General Orde Wingate - WC 15

## Public buildings
Brook Hospital - WC 11
Castlewood Centre - S 23
Clockhouse - W 42C
Fire Stations - W 37; P 45; S 28
Goldie Leigh Hospital - A 14
Greenwich & Bexley Hospice - A 13B
Magistrates Court - W 13
Memorial Hospital - S 4
Old Town Hall - W 15
Plumstead Library - P 43
Police Stations - W 13, 32E; S 1
Queen Elizabeth Hospital - WC 14
St Nicholas Centre - P 49
Shrewsbury House - S 29
Town Hall - W 11
Woolwich Library - W 15
Woolwich Post Office - W 3A

## Pubs
Abbey Arms - A 7
Admiral - W 47
Anglesea Arms - W 8
Army House - WC 25
Bull - W 4; S 19A
California - W 32G

## 96 - INDEX

Coopers Arms - W 24
Crown & Cushion - W 34
Director General - W 10
Dover Castle - P 3
Duke of Cambridge - W 79
Earl of Chatham - W 18
Edinburgh Castle - W 48
Foresters Arms - A 18
Fort Tavern - W 75
Fox & Hounds - W 68
Gatehouse - W 42B
Harrow Inn - A 6
Horse & Groom - P 42
Lord Clyde - W 66
Lord Derby - P 5
Lord Herbert - S 33A
Lord Raglan - W 84
Melbourne Arms - W 73
Navy & Army - W 47
Old Mill - P 26
Ordnance Arms - W 26
Plume of Feathers - P 41
Prince Albert - P 28
Prince of Orange - P 42
Prince of Wales - P 15
Prince Rupert - P 6
Pullman - W 29
Red Lion - P 48; S 21
Rose Inn - P 10
Royal Pavilion - W 32C
Ship - P 23
Thames Barrier Arms - W 60
Victoria - W 57
Volunteer - P 44
Walpole Arms - W 63
We Anchor in Hope - S 14
Who'd a Thought it - P 32
Woodman - P 36
Woolwich Infant - W 27

### Schools, colleges etc

Alexander McLeod School - A 12
Christ Church School - S 2
Conway School - P 53
Eglinton School - S 36
Foxhill Centre - W 67
Greenslade School - P 31
Plumcroft School - P 21
Plumstead Manor School - P 27
St Margarets School - P 14
St Marys School - W 39
St Patricks School - P 55
St Pauls School - A 16
South Rise School - P 8
Timbercroft School - P 34
University of Greenwich - W 17
Woodhill School - W 43
Woolwich College - W 61; P 3
Woolwich Polytechnic Schools - W 20, 78

### Streets

Abbey Wood Road - A 8, 9
Anglesea Road - W 6, 7
Barge House Road - W 32F
Beresford Square - W 26
Bloomfield Road - W 78, 79
Brewery Road - P 8, 9, 50, 51
Brookhill Road - W 63, 64, 66
Burrage Place - W 74
Burrage Road - W 81-84
Calderwood Street - W 14-17
Conduit Road - W 77
Crescent Road - W 76
Eaglesfield Road - S 16, 17, 28
Edge Hill - W 69
Eglinton Hill - S 27, 32
Frances Street - W 47
Frederick Place - W 74
General Gordon Place - W 2, 3
Genesta Road - P 20, 21
Griffin Road - P 55, 56
Herbert Road - S 33-35
Hillreach - W 45
Little Heath - W 50
Market Street - W 12, 13
McBean Street - W 20
Old Mill Road - P 26-29
Plum Lane - P 19
Plumstead Common Road - W 67-71, 80; P 15, 18, 23
Plumstead High Street - P 41-45, 48
Plumstead Road - W 27, 28; P 2, 3
Powis Street - W 19, 22, 23
Red Lion Lane - S 22
Repository Road - WC 16-18, 21-23
Rippolson Road - P 42
Rushgrove Street - WC 24
Samuel Street - W 48
Sandy Hill Road - W 72, 73, 75
Shooters Hill - S 1-3, 12, 13, 15, 18-21, 23
Shrewsbury Lane - S 24-26
The Slade - P 36, 37
Thomas Street - W 3A, 18
Timbercroft Lane - P 32-35
Tormount Road - P 30
Vernham Road - P 17
Walmer Terrace - P 4, 5
Waverley Crescent - P 11, 25
Waverley Road - P 10
Wellington Street - W 10, 11
White Hart Road - P 46, 47
Wickham Lane - A 16, 18
Woodhill - W 43, 44
Woodland Terrace - W 52, 53
Woodrow - W 46
Woolwich High Street - W 23-25, 33, 34
Woolwich Manorway - W 32F
Woolwich New Road - W 8-9, 26B, 29; WC 4
Wrottesley Road - P 16